JOSH FLAGG'S
THE DEAL

[51 FOR ME, 49 FOR YOU]

JOSH FLAGG'S

THE DEAL

[51 FOR ME, 49 FOR YOU]

///

SECRETS *for* MASTERING *the* ART *of* NEGOTIATION

HarperCollins
LEADERSHIP

An Imprint of HarperCollins

Published by HarperCollins Leadership, an imprint of HarperCollins Focus LLC.

Any internet addresses, phone numbers, or company or product information printed in this book are offered as a resource and are not intended in any way to be or to imply an endorsement by HarperCollins Leadership, nor does HarperCollins Leadership vouch for the existence, content, or services of these sites, phone numbers, companies, or products beyond the life of this book.

The views, thoughts, and opinions expressed in this book belong solely to the author in his personal capacity. Bravo, NBCUniversal, and their affiliates have not endorsed or otherwise been involved in this publication.

ISBN 978-1-4002-3044-0 (eBook)
ISBN 978-1-4002-3043-3 (HC)

Library of Congress Cataloging-in-Publication Data
Library of Congress Cataloging-in-Publication application has been submitted.

Printed in the United States of America
22 23 24 25 26 LSC 10 9 8 7 6 5 4 3 2 1

To Andrew.

You put the biggest smile on my face every day.

I love you more than words.

CONTENTS

———— /// ————

PART ONE
Don't Sell Garbage

PART TWO
You Have Only One Client

PART THREE
Up Your Attitude

PART FOUR
Be the Billionaire

PART FIVE
When to Say No

PART SIX
Know the Playing Field

PART SEVEN
Don't Let Little Problems Affect Big Deals

PART EIGHT
Play the Psychologist

PART NINE
Never Take the First Offer

PART TEN
Realize Your Worth

FOREWORD

———— /// ————

It's not every day that your former enemy and competitor for the last decade asks you to write the foreword to his book. It's also not often that you become best friends with the person you previously spent years trying to destroy. I did it all—stole his clients, took over his listings, and capitalized on every opportunity I had to make him look bad on television. With that being said, the world of real estate is strange and so is my dear friend Josh Flagg.

When I first met Flagg, I thought he was another spoiled, silver-spoon, Beverly Hills born-and-raised rich kid. Someone who was handed huge business without ever having to work for it. From working against him to now working with him, I've come to the realization that I was wrong and that his success is truly derived from his impressive work ethic, charisma, and industry expertise.

Through watching Flagg's approach in listing appointments, showings and negotiations, I have gotten a glimpse into the way his eccentric mind works and have come to understand his massive success. The Beverly Hills born-and-raised spoiled trust fund kid persona is actually just an act. In reality, Flagg is a confident and calculated real estate historian of Beverly Hills.

The best part of being friends with Flagg is seeing the way he runs his business. First, he will become best friends with an eighty-five-year-old woman through negotiations on her home. Right after, he will go to the Polo Lounge at the Beverly Hills Hotel to have a power lunch with a Hollywood music executive. Once he wraps up there, he's off to Spago for dinner with a tech billionaire. And, yes, he still finds enough time to get his hair done in his backyard while drinking white wine. A true businessman.

Josh Flagg may make the business look easy but don't think for a second that he is not trying. There's no question as to how he is a top-producing real estate agent. He will disarm you, charm you, become your best friend, and before you know it, you've accepted his offer. Believe it or not, I've learned a lot from Flagg and so can you. Competition is imperative for success as very few of us can motivate ourselves alone. I'd like to think part of my success is due to Flagg, my competition, for whom I will always be forever grateful.

JOSH ALTMAN
star of *Million Dollar Listing Los Angeles*

Welcome to Your Million-Dollar Mindset

Do you want to become a million-dollar dealmaker?

If your answer is an emphatic *"Hell, yes!"* then this is the book for you.

(If your answer is *"Not really!"* then why are you even in a bookstore? Shouldn't you be at a monster truck rally or something?)

For those of you who don't hate money or success, I've been closing multimillion-dollar deals since I was old enough to drive. I've sold $2.5 billion worth of luxury property, and I'm among the top three real estate agents in all Los Angeles and eighteenth in the nation.

What does this mean? It means that if I cared about sports—and I do not—I could get front row seats at the Lakers.

My client list includes all the other folks you'd see on the sidelines at the Staples Center. I'm talking about A-list celebrities like Shonda Rhimes, Adam Levine, Katy Perry, and Steve Aoki, and high-profile families like the Gettys, Bloomingdales, and DeBartolos. My sales have been recognized by the *Wall Street Journal*, and I've appeared on the *Forbes* "30 Under 30" list of the most influential people in their industry.

My prowess also landed me a starring role on *Million Dollar Listing Los Angeles*, and I built all this by myself, starting at age sixteen, without a college degree. (Well, I did come from a rich family, but that doesn't sound as good.)

"Cool résumé, Flagg," you may say. "But how does this help me get those seats at the game?"

The good news is, you don't need to be a realtor to benefit from the secrets of my success in negotiating multimillion-dollar deals. Whatever you sell, and regardless of what your negotiations may entail, applying my advice will up your game.

Do you want LeBron to sweat on your courtside seat? Because this can be yours with some effort.

That's why I'm going to walk you through what I do, how I do it, and why I do it. Spoiler alert: it's always about the money, but there's more to it as well. Anyone who tells you differently is a damn liar.

Follow me and I'll help uncover the strategies to cultivate your own powerful million-dollar dealmaker mindset. Whether you're looking for advice on negotiating a seven-plus-figure deal, hoping to demonstrate your worth to get that raise, or trying to woo that hot person at the club, I'm here to guide you.

Let's get ready to *werk*.

PART ONE

/ / /

Don't Sell Garbage

For every good listing, product, idea, you name it, there are ten crappy projects begging to be sold. We've all heard the mantra beggars can't be choosers; I stand by that 100 percent. So don't be a beggar . . . it's not chic.

Treat every sale like your reputation is on the line and that one lousy project will make it or break It.

ONE

///

Let's Talk About Sets, Baby

I'm successful beyond my wildest dreams because of my million-dollar mindset.

"Sounds great, Flagg," you might say. "But can you skip to the part where you tell us how to make more money?"

Truth is, we can't accomplish anything without the proper mindset. If you want more out of life than SpaghettiOs and time spent on the couch, let's dig into the concept of a mindset.

So . . . what's a mindset and why does it matter?

The best way to describe a mindset is that it's how we think about ourselves. Per Brett Steenbarger in *Forbes*: "Mindsets are an important means through which we process and reprocess the events of our lives. That matters, because our processing ultimately shapes our emotional experience. Limits become challenges, and challenges become sources of opportunity and growth."

Translation: proper mindset = more earning potential.

Our mindsets comprise the beliefs and attitudes that guide us in making sense of the world and our relationship to it. A mindset is dynamic and ever changing, so if you currently have, say, a losing or defeatist mindset, my goal is to help you alter it. Because SpaghettiOs can be okay in a pinch, but have you ever tasted La Scala's spaghetti Bolognese?

Carol Dweck, a researcher at Stanford University, studied the habits of extraordinarily successful people and discovered that we can transform our mindsets through effort, learning, and persistence. You want to trade up? Because this is how you trade up.

Quite simply, when we change our thinking, we change our outcomes.

I adopted a million-dollar mindset early on in my life. For me, the status quo has never been enough. No matter how good I am at something, I feel compelled to push myself past my limits. I won't approach an opportunity with a casual "whatever" attitude because then I'll stagnate or get bored. I refuse to accept a "meh, it's fine" mindset, and so should you.

Establishing a million-dollar mindset is all about raising your game to the next level. You don't have to be brokering luxury houses to follow this advice because the million-dollar mindset can apply to any sale or negotiation. If what you do involves a mutually accepted result, whether it's a handshake agreement or a hundred-page contract that entails sign-off from the entire legal department at your S&P 500 company, my advice will assist you in closing that deal. (Please note: for now, I'm using the terms "making deals" and "selling" interchangeably. We'll get into the subtle differences later.)

The main rules for establishing a million-dollar mindset are:

- You must be looking for something bigger and better than what you currently have.
- You must be willing to work to make it happen.

Here's an example of how I've used the mindset: Early in my real estate career, I was negotiating a deal where my sellers wanted $7.5 million for their home, but the buyer was stuck at $7.45 million. While the $7.5 million was the fair price, I broke into a cold sweat, panicking that I'd lose the sale over that $50,000 breach. And when would I get the opportunity to sell such a high-ticket property again?

I knew the most expedient way to close the deal would be to kick back $50,000 out of my commission and just be done with it. Honestly, I was tempted, but the mindset stopped me. I realized that while giving up a piece of the commission I'd worked for and rightfully earned was one solution, that strategy would never take me to the next level as a broker. Additionally, if I got a reputation for giving in at the beginning of my career, I'd forever be known as the kind of guy who caves under pressure. I needed to figure out how to make that pressure work for me, not against me. (You know what pressure can create? That's right, *diamonds*.)

While there are extenuating circumstances when a bit of a compromise can salvage a deal, in this case, and because of my mindset, the commission kickback was the wrong move.

My fear of losing the whole sale prevented me from best serving my seller and fighting for the proper asking price. I had to find a can't-lose way of processing my thoughts where I assured myself of my worth and abilities.

What I needed was to remove my emotions from the equation, specifically my fears.

I took an analytical look at what I'd already achieved at a young age, contrasting my successes to my failures. One column was demonstrably weightier than the other. That's not feeling; it's fact.

I posited that if I continued to work as hard and smart as I'd been, I was sure to produce hundreds of multimillion-dollar listings over the course of my career. If I lost this deal in fighting for it, I'd gain a reputation as the fight-for guy, not the give-in guy. As that rep grew, listings would come find me. I envisioned a future where I'd have so much business, all I'd have to do was say, "Next."

Instead of assuming my potential sales were a scarcity, I decided they'd be an abundance.

Thus, the million-dollar-dealmaker mindset was put in motion.

At this point, I'd done a few deals, so I drew on my limited experience. I already knew that when working with wealthy clients in the high-end market, people never walk away because of emotions.

This advice transcends the real estate market.

If the buyers want the property (or the car/watch/baby beluga) and they intended to close from the start, they will close. Period. What has made them wealthy is not paying $7.5 million for a home they can get for $7.45 million. Asking for a better deal isn't personal; it's business. If they were willing to lose the deal over $50,000, then they were never serious in the first place and were looking for a way out. Good riddance, in that case.

Fortified by my new mindset, I went back to the other broker and said, "I know how much your clients want this house, but my seller isn't budging from their final price of $7.5 million. Are you really going to advise your buyers to walk away, start over, and find another place they describe as their 'dream home' over a $50,000 disparity? How much is their time worth, especially when your clients have been looking for six months! That makes no sense. They need to take this deal as offered or they will lose this home."

Facts. Not feelings.

I closed the deal at $7.5 million. And guess what? The other broker kicked in the fifty thousand. (Hey, I don't care where it comes from as long as it isn't me.) The million-dollar mindset worked! Plus, being a tough negotiator in this instance taught me to weed out the real buyers from those who might be throwing out a low price just to see if it could stick.

For me, the million-dollar mindset is a combination of a positive attitude, coupled with successful behaviors and strategies, enhanced with a personal philosophy geared towards winning with integrity. (Outstanding personal style optional, but encouraged.)

A million-dollar-dealmaker mindset is more than a shortcut to creating successful outcomes or just a way to approach your business; it can apply to your whole life.

By cultivating this mindset, I've become wealthier than I ever imagined, and not just rich.

What's the difference?

Chris Rock explained it best in his 2004 comedy special, saying, "Shaq is rich, but the man who signs his checks is wealthy." (Note: Shaq has since cultivated wealth, thanks in part to savvy real estate investing.)

The world has changed since fictional financier Gordon Gekko proclaimed, "Greed is good!" in the seminal film *Wall Street*. Don't misunderstand me: the ability to go, do, and purchase what I want is a sheer delight—I won't lie and say it isn't. Money can't buy happiness, but it sure can lease it long term. Do I get a small thrill when I look around and see that I'm worth more than anyone in the room, especially at my age? Oh, I think you can guess my answer. (Do I sound proud? If so, it's because I've earned that right.)

However, the benefits of having resources extend far beyond an impressive line of credit. Financial security affords me the freedom to make choices and the clout to influence change . . . and it will do the same for you. As the descendant of Holocaust survivors, and with anti-Semitism on the rise in this country, I believe it's imperative to devote a healthy chunk of my earnings to Jewish causes like the Holocaust Museum LA and Cedars-Sinai. Giving back to my community is the most significant thing I'll ever do, and I use my privilege wisely.

Never again, indeed.

Now, let's start cultivating a million-dollar-dealmaker mindset that will create your own potentially world-changing financial resources.

Personally, I started in the industry by shadowing a real estate expert. I wish I could take on every eager learner as an intern, but that's not practical as my car isn't that big.

Instead, what I can do is to bring you along for the figurative ride in this book, offering up a rare inside look at how I operate, sharing the insights and advice that put me on the map by walking you through a typical twenty-four hours in my life. More importantly, I'll elaborate on the psychology behind a successful negotiation, making the advice evergreen for everyone whose bottom line depends on getting to yes. If your business entails people, expectations, or transactions, I'll help you manage them all.

With that, I invite you to join me. Please, spend the day in my shoes. Not literally, of course—you probably can't afford them now.

But follow my advice and you will.

TWO

The Ten-Thousand-Hour Rule

The first thing to know about me is that I don't sleep; I'm basically a great white shark in that I must keep moving for my buccal pumpers to—wait, I'm on Bravo, not the Discovery Channel. Regardless, that's why I'm writing this at 3:48 a.m.

My point is, I have far too many things to accomplish in a day to stay in bed for eight full hours. I must keep swimming. I'm lucky that I can operate on an abbreviated resting schedule—many can't (I think they're called "mammals") and that's apparently "normal."

Anyway, I'm not advocating that the key to success is to mainline caffeine and stumble around like a zombie. Dangerous mistakes happen when you're overtired. I suspect the Blockbuster executive who turned down the offer to buy Netflix was sleepwalking through his or her day. I'm sure that person loses a lot more sleep now.

Of course, my never napping was problematic when I was growing up. My poor mother! To get a break, she'd strap me into a car seat in the back of her black-on-tan SL convertible and drive me around Los Angeles to look at the gates in front of mansions. She found that viewing luxury real estate was the only way to placate me.

The second thing to know is that I'm a master dealmaker because I'm literally obsessed with selling homes. I'm not one of those oily guys who'd be content to hawk anything from pork bellies and soybean futures to software. I never want to be in a boiler room, sweating in a bad suit while cold calling about penny stocks; it's just not chic. That's not to say that you can't be a great salesperson by selling a product you're not passionate about, but you need to be passionate about at least one aspect of the deal. Whether it's the challenge of finding new buyers, the need to one-up the rest of the salespeople in your division, or just winning the approval of your peers and your family, you must be able to pinpoint what drives you to keep selling and lean into that.

For me, I'm wild about what I do because of the real estate. The ardor for my industry drives me. The love of the game keeps me awake at night. (Well, that and my late night calls with Candy Spelling where we watch *Columbo* together.) I'm passionate about every step of the buying and selling process—from seeing the property for the first time, to landing the listing, to showcasing the home's potential, to getting my clients the absolute best deal.

Selling high-end real estate is not only my job but, it can be argued, it is my destiny.

In his book *Outliers*, Malcolm Gladwell describes what he calls the ten-thousand-hour rule. He posits that while success doesn't come without innate talent, a lucky break, or a degree of privilege (oh, hello), the underpinning to achievement lies in having spent ten thousand hours mastering the task at hand. He uses Bill Gates to illustrate this example.

Yes, Gates had the natural aptitude to be a great computer programmer, but what pushed him forward was engaging in ten-thousand hours of *actual* computer programming before he went to college. Gates grew up close to a University of Washington campus, and as a teen, he'd head down the street to spend all night in the computer labs. Because his parents supported his interest, they donated computers to his private school. (I have to say it again—rich parents are *the best*. Let's work on making you one for your kids.) Ergo, by the time he arrived at Harvard, Gates had thousands of hours of access that most didn't have in that era.

Can you imagine how Gates must flex now, all, "Yeah, my Gulfstream G650 is cool, but have you ever eradicated malaria from an entire continent, brah?"

While some researchers assert that practicing/learning a skill for ten thousand hours is an oversimplification to explain success, in my case, it's true. As a little boy, I began constructing a Lego universe, a fabulous mixed-use development, complete with a shopping promenade and helicopter pad. I spent years adding to the structure. Woe to any housekeeper who tried to vacuum around it. (Right, I could be a pint-sized tyrant, thanks for noticing.) Given my dedication, my parents assumed I'd grow up to be an architect or a Marvel supervillain. (I was the first to master a land lease because I didn't own the property below those Lego buildings—my parents did—but I still built those skyscrapers.)

During this same time, I also had a dollhouse my grandmother Edith bought for me. She didn't say, "Well, this is a little gay," when we saw it in the toy store. Instead, she agreed it was genuinely nice and that someone had clearly put a lot of effort into building it. She didn't care about traditional gender roles; her only concern was craftsmanship. I never actually played with dolls, though. I spent all my time filling it with antiques and furniture, so . . . a little gay.

I was also obsessed with house keys at that age. To me, keys represented freedom and opportunity, and I wanted both so badly. When friends and neighbors gathered at our family home, my dad warned guests to hide their keys because I'd run off with them. For those who assumed he was kidding, I'd swipe the keyrings out of their pockets and let myself into their houses later—not to steal anything, just to look around. I suspect everyone's glad I didn't grow up to be a cat burglar, even though that does sound chic in the Thomas Crown sense.

I was so infatuated with certain homes that I convinced my mother to knock on neighborhood doors with me, asking strangers if we might peek inside. What's crazy is that people often agreed! Who does that? I want to say I was a master negotiator even then, but the more likely explanation is that a bowl-cut six-year-old in a Le Petit Prince turtleneck is inherently nonthreatening.

Those early tours instilled a deep and abiding love for luxury real estate. Scoring the coup of a private showing of my grandparents' friends the Blacks' house on Sunset was a dream come true. This palatial residence, its lawn dotted with bronze sculptures, was formerly owned by Howard Hughes. Judy Garland once lived there too. Touring it was a visit through Los Angeles history.

I'm thankful to have grown up with my parents, Michael and Cindy, who encouraged my eccentricities rather than tried to discipline them out of me. (I like to say the difference between "weird" and "eccentric" is a few commas in a bank balance.) Anyway, it would have been easy for them to mistake my enthusiasm for disobedience; but they didn't, and I love them all the more for it.

I attended the Catskills West theater camp at historic Greystone Mansion in Trousdale Estates in Beverly Hills, the Doheny family–built Tudor revival mansion that may be the greatest property on the entire West Coast. You might recognize the exterior from being featured in *The Big Lebowski*, *Gilmore Girls*, and *The Witches of Eastwick*.

While I was a decent actor and I liked camp, I was far more intrigued by the majestic residence and its scandalous history. Owner and oil heir Ned Doheny died just months after he and his family moved into the estate in 1929. His body was found in a guest room in what appeared to be a murder-suicide with his secretary and "dear friend" (cough, cough) Hugh Plunkett. When Doheny's wife heard the first gunshot, she called the family's doctor and not the police. Rumor has it, she was the one to pull the trigger, as she didn't fancy her husband being a little light in the loafers . . . if you know what I mean. Whatever the story, this is exactly the kind of fishy behavior that podcasts—and curious eight-year-olds—love to unpack.

Back then, I began to draw my dream home based on the architectural renderings of Greystone. I even had my father get me a Sotheby's catalog of the late Jacqueline Kennedy Onassis's estate when it came to auction. I pored over every page, picking out which of her pieces I'd want to fill my stately manor. Not sure how I'd planned to scrape together enough allowance to buy Jackie O's silver monogrammed tape measure she'd used to estimate the future White House drapes, but I assumed I'd find a way. (Spoiler alert: I did not find a way, as this item sold to an interior designer for just shy of $50,000. I remain salty about it, and I still browse the catalog to this day.)

Occasionally at Catskills West, I'd wander away from the other campers, and the counselors would find me showing off the property to European visitors, breathlessly describing the Indiana limestone and Welsh slate roof. Ask me how happy my mother was when she found out I'd gotten in a car with a pack of German tourists.

So, why didn't those tourists question having a child tour guide, you might ask?

Because I was so well informed. Skills trump age every time.

Suffice it to say, I'd put in my ten thousand hours long before I started shaving.

FLAGG THIS

What are your passions?

What are you naturally predisposed to selling?

Where have you acquired ten thousand hours of experience?

What product, service, or idea would excite you so much, you'd lose sleep over the anticipation of starting your day?

Make a list of the areas where you're considered an expert and target potential employment in those industries. For example, you grew up playing tennis but lacked the skill to go pro—imagine the credibility you'd bring to the table selling for a racquet manufacturer like Wilson. Or if you've been leading the charge for recycling since childhood—how satisfying would it be to negotiate contracts for a clean energy company?

Remember, buyers respond to enthusiasm, especially when coupled with expertise. Capitalize on this and reap the results.

THREE

///

525,600 Minutes

My day begins at 7:30 a.m., even though I was awake until 4:00 a.m. as I'd been chatting with Candy before designing tablescapes for an upcoming dinner party. I undertook this task because I was too excited about what's to come this evening to even consider sleep. (More on that later.)

Olimpia, my housekeeper, greets me with coffee and a couple poached eggs, some very thinly sliced rye toast, and smoked salmon, the exact breakfast Edith ate every morning. This is the last thing I remember to consume until my dinner date with destiny.

The front yard is a hive of activity. When I say *hive*, I mean it. Recently, *Real Housewives of New York*'s Sonja Morgan showed up for an unexpected weekend visit. When she finally departed two weeks and thousands of dollars' worth of water damage later, dozens of bees appeared outside the guest room window. While I'm concerned the swarm coupled with the flooding may be the signs of the coming apocalypse, I have more important things to worry about today.

Olimpia buzzes in Mark, the stylist who's done my hair since I was thirteen. I'm filming bites—the talking head segments between the action—for *Million Dollar Listing* today, and I need to be camera-ready.

This is the first of many timesaving moments of my day.

Yes, I'm capable of drying my hair myself; it's grooming, not Euclidian geometry. But my success is partially predicated on time carved from the hundreds of efficiencies I've created over the years. Time is a nonrenewable resource. In this case, I can style myself or I can have Mark do it while I use those extra few minutes to complete tasks that will bring in more business. (Okay . . . maybe I look like Donald Trump when I do it myself, but still.)

Obviously, in-home haircare isn't something most can consider, especially when first starting out, but the notion of not wasting time is scalable. In the words of DJ Quik, "If it don't make dollars, it don't make sense." Learn to live by that motto, proper grammar optional.

Once, a millionaire developer client mentioned to me that he'd changed his own oil in his car over the weekend. "Was that something you enjoyed?" I asked, as he didn't seem the type to get his hands dirty. "No," he replied with a terse laugh. "It was frustrating and difficult and took my whole Saturday."

I didn't need to remind him of what he might have accomplished instead in the time he'd wasted trying to DIY—he was well aware.

FLAGG THIS

I consider the "pleasure principle" when structuring my day. Time is precious. I devote my free moments only to what I love or to what makes me happy. For example, I could outsource my tabletop designs, but I don't want to because a beautiful, elegant place setting is one of the ways I make my guests feel welcome and special.

What do you want to have more time to do and what areas can you streamline to create it?

With the *Cabaret* soundtrack on in the background, I tweak a marketing document. My assistant Claire, a no-nonsense Jersey girl, perches on the side of the tub as we run through my relentless schedule. Claire is an invaluable part of the pit crew that keeps my day on track. She knows how much I hate to be idle, and she makes it her job to not waste a second. I move the conversation forward by saying "Next!" each time we complete a task. That she's never (yet) shanked me for barking "Next!" speaks to her equanimity.

From my bathroom vista, I spy landscapers swatting bees while an automotive service washes the cars in the semicircular drive. A different team pulls up in a tanker truck to refuel all the vehicles in the drive. I know, I know—gardeners and live-in staff and on-call glam squads sound aspirational, but damn it, not pumping my own gas goes too far. Yet I argue that having fuel brought to me costs only a few extra bucks a month. My dad does this thing where he'll take his Range Rover all the way across town to save $20 on a tank of gas, even though it costs him forty minutes of time. It makes me crazy!

Again, while I can't buy more hours in the day, I can ante up the resources to maximize the minutes I do have. I've never forgotten when I missed out on a listing opportunity because I ran late, having stopped at Jack Colker's Union 76 station first. I blew what could have been a $100,000 commission by not forking out the $20 for this service. Bit of a false economy, eh?

FLAGG THIS

Reflect on your typical workday. Where can you create efficiencies? How can you maximize your time?

Could you eke out an extra twenty minutes to research leads if you took an Uber to the office instead of driving yourself?

Might you complete an additional proposal if you hire a neighbor to supervise your kids' homework during that chaotic time after school and before dinner?

Sometimes, a few dollars can make the difference in reaching the next level in your career.

Hair complete, Claire collects the marketing collateral we'll need for our first appointment while I dress. She often rides with me while I'm out on appointments, taking notes and connecting calls. Later today, we're interviewing an assistant for her as the workload is ever increasing as my business expands.

Choosing an outfit is quick. I also keep a look book of all my clothing, divided into tabs such as "Listing Appointment" and "Weekend in Montecito" and "Poolside Gossip." I pick jeans, Gucci sneakers, and a simple black V-neck cashmere sweater. I'm a fourth-generation Angeleno on my mom's side of the family, so my blood is thin, and it's sweater weather for me until it hits eighty degrees.

We pull out of the drive, waving goodbye to the staff (and the growing colony of bees), and we're off to a listing appointment in the Wilshire Corridor area.

My first phone call is with my friend Rick Caruso, who may well be the next mayor of Los Angeles. (It never hurts to have fancy friends, if for no reason other than to say, "Sorry, Warren Beatty's on the other line—gotta go.") However, our chat is cut short when the *Wall Street Journal* calls. The reporter wants my take on the viability of a new development in Century City. I establish my credibility by starting the conversation with my knowledge of my grandmother Edith's old penthouse on Avenue of the Stars. She'd purchased it from Hollywood icon Jack Benny for the highest price recorded for a condo in LA as of 1976.

My answers are upbeat and well informed, as that's exactly how I want the press to view me. I jump on every opportunity to tout my knowledge and expertise.

FLAGG THIS

I am never not selling, even when I don't have a deal to close. Every part of my life broadcasts and reinforces the notion of success, from what I drive to the lighting on the floral display outside my house.

Ultimately, you are your product, and you must present yourself accordingly.

Remember, you don't have to be rich to be polished, professional, and proactive, but these factors will help you get there.

While we drive, Claire rolls calls. When I'm working, there are no distractions. We don't zone out and gossip or listen to podcasts, although sometimes we'll stream some calming yacht rock in the background. If I have a free second, I'm on the phone, answering calls or checking in with clients. Or maybe I'm coming up with a caption for a social media post or pitching a new partnership. While I'm never frenetic—not chic—I use every second of my day. The converse is, I have no problem vacationing for an entire month in the summer. I love to work, but I don't *live* to work. Because I focus when I should, I'm able to unplug at will.

Without balance, burnout is assured.

Next call is with the *New York Post*. They're seeking details behind my sale of Suzanne Somers's house, a massive Palm Springs compound that *People* magazine called "legendary." Oh, they are not wrong. Somers bought the sprawling property with her husband, Alan Hamel, in the late 1970s as a refuge from the constant barrage of paparazzi during her *Three's Company* heyday. The house sat on the market for years—literally—until I took over.

I was psyched to represent the couple as their decades-long marriage is as awe-inspiring as the property itself. Almost no one has that kind of track record in Hollywood. Plus, everything about those twenty-eight acres spoke to me, from the natural rock walls in the private guest cottages to the hidden wine cellar. And, hello—there's a hillside tram! Who else can say they have their own funicular? I love that word by the way. So rich.

I fell in love instantly and couldn't wait to put the Flagg name on the property. I wasn't even out of the driveway before I started calling potential buyers. With a fresh strategy including updated pricing and a coordinated marketing push . . . sold!

The key to making the deal happen was in passing up other lucrative listings. I needed to ensure that Somers and Hamel would get the full benefit of my attention. I never spread myself too thin. Making a sale to a buyer is a short-term gain, while cultivating a loyal client is a long-term investment in the future. And I'd rather have one happy client than ten unhappy buyers.

You see, I run my business by treating every sale like my reputation is on the line and that one inferior project could make or break it; you should, too.

———— /// ————

FOUR

Garbage?
Nope, Don't Sell It

What makes me a multimillion-dollar sales negotiator?

One of the factors is my refusal to sell garbage.

Does that mean I wouldn't consider listing a home for less than $10 million? Of course not! I don't judge a property based on a price point. I've been as happy selling condos for $800,000 as I have been with $40 million estates.

Two things to note here before I continue: if you live anywhere but Los Angeles, San Francisco, or New York, $800,000 can buy you a freaking palace, with turrets and everything. Not in this town. Here, you might get a one-bedroom condo with a view of a dumpster.

The second thing is, while the disparity between $800,000 and $40 million sounds like a huge gap, what those homes had in common is that I believed in them. I wanted to represent them because they also represented me. So when I'm on a listing appointment, the seller isn't the sole party deciding whether to move forward.

I understand that dealmakers don't always have a choice, but if you are able to choose, choose wisely. Elect to sell what speaks to you, even if it's more effort on the front end. Set yourself up for future success by picking products, services, or ideas you'd be proud to represent.

Honestly, I'd rather list an historically interesting home for $1.5 million than I would a generic white box building for $15 million. That's why I began my career swinging for the fences. I wanted to be a luxury realtor, so I pursued only luxury listings. (While successful, the strategy wasn't perfect, but more on this soon.)

At sixteen, I knew I was born to sell real estate. I wasn't about to waste two more years until graduation and then another four in college to get started; I wanted those metaphorical keys *now*. While my peers fretted about acing the SATs, I fast-forwarded my own future.

The biggest broker at the time was a possibly litigious man I'll call Mr. Mentor. Mr. Mentor was the guy you called if you were rich, famous, and looking for a luxury property. He'd been the real estate king for decades. I admired how he always took out pages upon pages of full-page ads in every publication for his clients' $20 million properties, so I wanted to intern with him.

I came up with a plan that may or may not have involved some light stalking.

I knew who Mr. Mentor was because I was in a golf clinic at Hillcrest Country Club with a kid whose dad had bought an incredibly famous house from him. I "bumped into" him one day at Hillcrest. To pique his interest, I told him that my parents were looking to buy a home he'd listed. (Listen, I don't advocate lying now. But I was sixteen and wore a lot of trucker caps. Not every judgment call I made back then was perfect.) My parents even played along, and we got him to show us the house. They didn't purchase the place, obviously, but I did get the internship.

In real estate sales, the best thing you can do is find the top person and offer up your services, free of charge. But keep your day job at first—you still need to eat. You'd be surprised at how many huge agents are amenable to this because they can use the help, and ultimately people love a bargain and "free" is the ultimate coup.

What's crucial about working under a major producer is the synergy you'll experience—you must be around people in the know. You must hear what's happening in the marketplace if you're going to truly understand it. So many people take the real estate classes, get their licenses, and then join, let's say, an entity like Coldwell Banker. They get thrown in the pit, and without any actionable experience, they flounder. Maybe if they're lucky, they'll get a listing from a family member or friend, but that's not sustainable. Don't try to do it on your own; you'll never make it. For example, in Los Angeles, there are about ten thousand licensees. Maybe a thousand of those people do any business. One hundred are successful, and ten do 99 percent of all that business.

FLAGG THIS

Before you start a real estate career/straight commission-based position, take an honest self-assessment.

Are you outgoing?

Are you interesting?

Are you gregarious?

Do you have the resources to sustain your lifestyle before you start making money? If not, are you willing to make sacrifices while you're learning?

If you answer no to any of these questions, this may not be the field for you.

Also, you must have evidence of your own charisma if you want a position where you influence how people spend their money on such a personal decision. That your nana thinks you're charming is not enough. (FYI, Edith found almost no one charming.)

What I didn't realize when I landed the internship was that Mentor's business was beginning to dry up. He'd handed off most of the responsibilities to his business partner, the Robin to Mentor's Batman, who'd eventually run the whole business off the rails, taking them from a Bel Air mansion to a shitty apartment on Fox Hills Drive.

Still, I'd sit by Mentor's side at open houses and on calls, and that education was inestimable. When we'd drive around Beverly Hills, he could recite every arcane bit of information about each home we passed. His knowledge was encyclopedic—he could tell me anyone who ever lived there, what they paid, and even what they still owed. His attention to detail floored me; he noticed and knew everything.

I eschewed my high school classes and instead studied the history of Beverly Hills and Bel Air. Could I tell you the past participle of the French verb *avoir*? *Mais non*. (Well, actually, I took Latin and *veni, vidi, vici* . . . I'm outta this school!) I could talk at length about what famous lothario used to own a property and which starlet was accosted there, and that information proved far more valuable. (Fatty Arbuckle, I'm looking at you.)

In this town, buyers are ravenous for a taste of history and a brush with fame, regardless of how sordid.

FLAGG THIS

Lots of salespeople find one-off success by employing hard-sell techniques. (Think "used car salesman.")

Set yourself apart by becoming a trusted advisor. Have the most information. Be more knowledgeable than your competition. Facts can be more powerful than feelings.

If you know everything and everyone, you will excel. If choose not to . . . you're an idiot.

In my first year as an intern, Robin and I managed to sell what had once been a $20 million listing. (Keep in mind, this was twenty years ago, when a $20 million dollar home was today's equivalent of $100 million.) Sheik Mohammad Al-Fassi had lived in this Italianate mansion built by Max Whittier, the cofounder of Beverly Hills. The sheik put his personal stamp all over it, you know, just super tasteful touches like adding pubic hair to nude statues and filling planters with plastic flowers in lurid colors like celadon and lime green. (I wish I were kidding, but

I can't make this shit up.) I'd invite you to imagine it, but you don't have to. This tacky palace was the set for Steve Martin's *The Jerk*. Remember the clam shell bathtub and the bordello room? My dear, those were *real*. No one was sorry when the previously glorious monstrosity burned down (by one of the neighbors, not surprisingly) in 1985, leaving a lot full of rubble. The lot was subdivided by the time that Robin and I got to it, and we sold one of the portions.

The most important thing I learned from Mentor was that when you buy a home, you're ultimately investing in the dirt it sits on. A home is worth only as much as where it's located. And a lot the size of the sheik's property was worth plenty. The possibilities for that space were endless! Said dirt ended up selling for $13 million, and I negotiated that deal on a Sidekick phone from my math class.

Did Mentor and Robin end up taking advantage of my naivete?

You bet they did.

Even when I sold a home on my own, they'd interject themselves into the deal and would weasel out a huge percentage of the sale. Plus, they'd pimp me out to their old gay friends to help them decorate, and those men would always ask for kisses.

It was almost creepy enough to make me turn straight.

Once, they sent me to Tahiti to take photos from a helicopter of an island we were marketing for sale. Okay, that part was cool, but the eighteen hours I spent in coach—both ways—was less so. They were so cheap they didn't pay for an extra night in a hotel, so I wasn't even there for a whole day. I didn't have a minute to order a tropical drink served in a coconut or one of those flaming pupu platters. (Still mad about it, FYI.)

All they did was take from me, giving me nothing in return . . . save for an inadvertent education. Turns out, that was enough. I wouldn't trade the experience for a four-year degree. I learned far more from the internship than I ever would have in college. So by the time I graduated from high school, I was ready to move on, get my own license, and find my own listings. I left them two years after I was licensed, rich only on the knowledge I'd gained.

One of my first acts was to wheedle the *Beverly Hills Courier* into running a feature about the budding high school real estate mogul. Ever the salesman, I told them I'd save them the time of interviewing me by simply writing up my talking points and sending them over. (Again, people are lazy—make it easy for them, respect their time, and reap the results.) The paper ran my self-penned article and my senior picture with the headline *BH Student Set to Make Records*. It was official; I was in the game.

FLAGG THIS

I t's never too soon to start being your own publicist.

I began my solo career knocking on doors in Beverly Hills. The very first person I met as an agent was Jay Bernstein, Suzanne Somers's publicist. And that brings us full circle back to the present. Isn't it ironic that I would end up selling Suzanne and Alan's home sixteen years later?

For as large as Los Angeles is, sometimes it's a small town.

///

FIVE

You Can't Sell It
If You Don't List It

Claire and I arrive at a condo building in the Wilshire Corridor, so I have to hang up with my friend Melissa Rivers. This area's super desirable, and it's often called the "Millionaire Mile," as it's surrounded by Beverly Hills, Holmby Hills, and Bel Air, set against a backdrop of spectacular views. Some refer to the area as the Gold Coast, as it reminds me of a retirement home in Miami. (Okay, it's me; I am "some.")

I've sold a ton of units on this block, thanks to the proximity to UCLA, the studios, and the 405 freeway, plus all the amenities each luxury building boasts. But this particular property is new to me—there aren't many recent sales in this building, which means that most residents have lived here longer term. That could be a real plus.

Claire and I pull into the underground parking facility where we're met by a valet. He tells us where to go and we pass through clean, spacious public areas with Venetian plaster finishes, arched doorways, and lots of marble, in design reminiscent of the Italian Riviera. Claire is on speakerphone scheduling time with one of the designers working on my new home, and I'm finishing a text as we take the elevator up to the penthouse. No second wasted.

Jayla, the owner, greets us as we exit the elevator. The moment we meet, she becomes my sole focus. Granted, I'm a huge proponent of multitasking, but when I'm with a potential client, that person is my only priority. In fact, when I'm face-to-face with a buyer or seller and my phone rings, I never pick it up. Instead, I'm preternaturally present. I actively listen and I watch for nonverbal cues. I restate the points they emphasize.

If I were to go into a meeting mentally rehearsing whatever I planned to say next, I wouldn't be fully attuned to what's being communicated. I pay attention to everything—even throwaway statements—as those can be so telling. As a broker, my job is to gather information, and I can't do it properly if I'm distracted. As an ad hoc therapist, I listen to every single word they say and use it to our mutual advantage when buying or selling their place.

FLAGG THIS

Be present when you're courting business.

No, be more than just present—be perpetually present. Put down your device. Throw it out the window, I don't care, just get rid of that distraction and focus on that moment and that moment only.

Listen to your potential client . . . they will reveal everything you need to know without realizing they're doing it. You often have only one shot to gather data, so use it!

Back to the condo because we're focusing on our potential client, Jayla. She ushers us in through the oversized front door, and we enter her four-bed, four-bath corner unit with lots of outdoor living space and views all the way to the ocean. The main living area is open-concept, and the windows take up two full walls. As we tour the condo, I make mental notes of all the best features, such as how the duplexed second floor has space to build an in-unit elevator, providing accessibility for a potentially older buyer.

After we're done assessing the property, we sit down to discuss the possibility of working together. The seller's decision to list ultimately hinges on a consensus on asking price. But long before we get to that conversation, I've posed dozens of other questions.

The questions I ask Jayla during our tour center on who she is. *What does she value? How does she live her life? What's important to her?* The more I know about a potential client, the more effective I can be as a broker. Many agents would take this time to talk about themselves, touting their sales and their brokerage and their expertise, but that's a rookie mistake. The initial conversation is the time for fact-finding, not an opening salvo hard sell.

With Jayla, I notice an easel and a box of oil paints by the sliding glass door. I want to find out about her painting—is she professional or just a hobbyist? Does she need more space for her art? Would living in a home with skylights or southern exposure appeal to her? This is a clever way of asking if she's looking to buy as she sells without coming across as oily or aggressive and putting her on the defensive. Also, I hope she isn't planning to make a living off her work, because I don't list any cardboard boxes by the freeway underpass. (I keep this opinion to myself, FYI.)

Questions answered, now it's time for the big dance—determining an asking price. Of course, I am intimately acquainted with how much comparative listings have sold for in the building and neighborhood. I live and breathe comps, and I'll come in with a well-informed number. However, I never offer my thoughts first because that's the surest way to lose a listing before I even get it. Here's the thing—no one knows exactly what a home is worth, so pricing is a bit of a game.

Or a mindfuck.

My strategy is to dig, to gauge what prices other brokers are telling them their home is worth *before* giving my opinion. I'll say something like, "Let me guess, they're telling you it's a (blank) dollar listing." I want to know what others have said before I commit to a number. I'll also ask, "What sold properties are you comparing your home with?" and a savvy seller will occasionally have an idea. But mostly they'll reply, "That's why you're here." They're not wrong, but this also makes it tougher, as it shows they aren't ready to reveal any information to me.

So often a client will go with the agent who tells them the highest number, and that's the shortsighted call because there's little proof the home can fetch that price. (Again, mindfuck.) Pricing a home too high initially is the kiss of death. The first few weeks on the market are the most important, so I always want a home to generate interest right out of the gate. Not gonna happen if it's priced too high.

I won't say an overpriced property never sells because some do surprise me, but it's not the norm. Honestly, it's better if a seller comes in a bit lower because that can spur a competitive bidding situation. Price it right and you'll get offers either at asking price or very close.

Jayla believes her home is worth $8 million, and so do the agents with whom she's spoken. Personally, I believe Jayla and the other agents are high AF. But again, not something I can say aloud.

The proposed price is easily $1 million above the comps, and those are better units in newer buildings with more amenities. When I run into this situation, I keep an ace up my sleeve. I call it The Brokers' Price Opinion, and we'll delve into those details in a later chapter.

Once Jayla and I have the potential price discussion out of the way, only then do I start to sell myself. I highlight my sales record and I detail the homes I've sold, pointing out that I represent all price points.

I walk the potential client through all the facets of my hands-on approach and each way I make myself available. Then I give them my phone number and explain how when they call me, they'll get *me*, not an assistant.

I've done this enough to know the questions a potential seller might have, and I address those concerns *before* he or she has a chance to raise them. The reaction I always get is, "I'm so glad you said something about that; I was worried." I find that when I provide answers to questions before they're asked, my answers are perceived as more credible.

No salesperson is flawless, but we can outmaneuver the competition by putting our foibles out there first. Salespeople can be hesitant to call out perceived weaknesses, hoping a client will gloss over or ignore them. That's the wrong move. When we're proactive about concerns, we come across as confident, not defensive. And honest!!

One of the most common objections I face is that I'm a one-man show. I change this perception by touting the benefits of individualized service. I show the value of not being ignored by a brokerage that's a huge, impersonal factory. I also give credit where it's due, and I mention all the people on my team who support me, specifically so I can be more available.

Like today, I often bring a support staff member with me, and I intentionally call all of them my "secretaries" so Claire or Hilary can stop and correct me, explaining that they're my *assistants*. This demonstrates that I am happy to defer when presented an appropriate challenge. (P.S. I would never call them my secretaries in real life—they would legit murder me. However, I won't lie; I do it all the time behind their backs.)

Of course, if I ever do bring on a team of agents under me, you can bet that I'll have a dozen reasons in my pitch why bigger is better.

FLAGG THIS

Make a list of your weaknesses or shortcomings. Call out what a potential customer might fixate on when you're sitting in front of them. Be brutally honest. Dig deep. Maybe have a mean friend help.

Practice turning those perceived negative traits into a benefit. This exercise is Real Estate 101. *It's not small—it's cozy. It's not underneath the train tracks—it's close to public transportation. It's not a murder house—it's historically significant.*

Perhaps in your case, you're not too young; instead, you have tons of energy. You're not too old; you have years of experience. You're not too green; instead, you're eager to learn and have a fresh perspective.

> Your flaws are never flaws—they're the features that make you unique. Spin them to your benefit.

In my opinion, a potential client meeting is successful when by the end of the appointment, the seller has no questions for me. If questions remain, I consider this a failure. I conclude my meetings by saying, "You should interview ten other agents. They're going to say what you want to hear and not what's best for your property."

I figure they're going to do it anyway but suggesting this puts me in control and makes them think it's my idea. It's all about being so proactive in my discussion points that I even beat them to their own thoughts. This immediately builds trust. I make it my job to interview the client, not vice versa, because it gives me the upper hand.

Jayla has nothing left to ask when I'm done talking, so we say our goodbyes. The listing is mine for the taking. One of my tricks is to never bring listing paperwork with me because this gives off big Used Car Salesman energy. If the seller wants to work with me, I'll make sure they know where to find me.

While this is a perfectly nice building and a perfectly nice unit in a desirable area where I've made tons of sales, I'm not excited about the listing. My pulse isn't racing. I'm not already scrolling through my contact list to call the perfect buyer. I'm not mentally staging photos of the unit for mailers. This place just isn't clicking for me.

As Claire and I exit, we're overwhelmed by the smell of Russian food in the hallway. (How did I miss that on the way in? It's like being slapped in the face with a bowl of borscht.)

The biggest factor here is that while Jayla agreed to a potential listing price in theory, she gave every indication that she wouldn't accept it in practice. I had the impression that if someone wanted to overpay her the $1 million she thought it was worth, sure, she'd consider an offer. But she wasn't serious about relocating; she was fishing for an unattainable price. I can tell you from experience that an uncommitted seller is a seller who will waste my valuable time.

No one can argue that an $8 million (really more like $7 million on a good day) duplexed penthouse in the Wilshire Corridor is "garbage." But for my purposes, any potential property that sucks up my time, effort, and marketing dollars with little potential for return on investment fits that definition.

Bottom line, I'm not excited to put my name on this listing. As a seller, Jayla deserves more from her broker than that. While it's not easy to walk away from a $125,000 to $150,000 potential commission, I'm not taking this listing because I don't sell garbage.

I check my voicemail as we walk to the car. While we were in Jayla's house, I received a call from a developer looking to see $20 million properties in the Hills and could I maybe meet with him this afternoon?

Next.

PART TWO

———— /// ————

You Have Only One Client

My clients want to feel like they're the only clients I have. Sometimes that means flying across the country to meet with them to sign papers when I could just as easily send papers by email or DocuSign.

Some dealmakers think reputation alone will buy them clients. And it can, to an extent. But keeping your clients is part of the game too. If I'm treating my client to a gourmet three-course dinner and champagne in L.A.'s finest watering hole after closing a successful deal, who wouldn't want to call me for the next project that comes along?

But before you can ever lavish service on your clients, you must find them.

So, let's do that first.

SIX

Selling Los Angeles

The Bravo network released a show called *Million Dollar Listing* in 2006. The initial iteration was . . . different. The show had the same production values as the HGTV house-flipping shows back then and didn't evoke the same luxury feel as present day.

I watched the show a few times—how could I not? They were filming in my backyard! I saw the potential of the program, but more important, I recognized the potential of *being* on it. I knew I handled more impressive homes than what I'd seen thus far, and I was convinced that I could be more entertaining than *that* cavalcade of corpses.

People assume *MDLLA* came looking for me—not true. Instead, I started making calls and got through to World of Wonder, the production company responsible for filming the show. I introduced myself and explained why I should interview with them to be on the next season. Listen, no one is going to come knocking on your door—you need to go after them!

Maybe they'd been scouting me, having seen my deals in the paper, but I wasn't leaving anything to chance. I was convinced I was the right fit, so when I decided to pitch them, I knew I could do as much for WOW as they could for me. While I wasn't brand new to the business, I ascertained that if done correctly, the show could open a floodgate of opportunities, and I wanted in.

I was bold, but I also had the chops to prove it. Landing the opportunity is never enough. When we score a chance based on our confidence, we must have the skills to back up our claims. We (well, not *me*, but sports people) still talk about when an at-bat Babe Ruth called his shot in game 3 of the 1932 World Series because he delivered the home run he'd promised.

No one recalls the guys who struck out that day.

Anyway, all I needed was ten minutes of the producers' time to convince them. I worked my magic on the phone and scored an interview. Those ten minutes I hoped for turned into an in-person ninety minutes, and at the end of them, I'd been cast. I got the call while lunching with my mom at Neiman Marcus—she was so proud!

When the second season of the show premiered in 2008, everything was different. The name had been changed to *Million Dollar Listing Los Angeles* and save for Madison, the previous cast members were gone.

Anyway, production values now mirrored that of other Bravo shows with slick transition shots, sophisticated music cues, and aspirational lighting. The featured real estate values—and some of the brokers' egos (okay, mine)—grew exponentially.

We'd created lightning in a bottle.

The takeaway here is, it wasn't enough for me to be confident that I was worthy. Who knows if World of Wonder might have come to find me? Instead, I used my sales skills to pitch my most valuable product—myself—and when the cameras started rolling and I needed to close deals?

That's exactly what I did.

Thanks to Bravo taking a chance on me, my next stop in what is a typical twenty-four-hour day for me is the World of Wonder studio. I'm not on location today; instead I'm filming the bites between segments.

I believe the show has maintained its popularity because of our interaction with our clients—we truly are focused on them, and the drama stems from our trying to please them. These are real situations, with millions of dollars on the line with each transaction. Also, the real estate porn doesn't hurt.

I juggle calls the entire short drive there. I briefly shoot the shit with Heather Altman, Josh Altman's wife, and then I speak with a couple coagents for a major estate we're representing. I also follow up with the private investigator I hired to track down a former client who violated the terms of our listing agreement. (Word of advice? Don't violate the terms of our listing agreement.)

Today's filming entails me interrupting my friend and fellow castmate Tracy Tutor's bites to surprise her. I'd recently represented her in buying a new home, and I ended up giving up my commission to get her into her dream house. Today, I surprised her with the news and a set of keys. There are messy tears, and I make a mental note to discuss her eye makeup choices later.

Start to finish takes less than an hour and then I'm done filming for the day. So, when I promise my clients that the show won't keep me from managing their listings, I'm not kidding. I head back to my car, sans crew this time, and get on with my day.

Even though I'm $200,000 less rich than I should be, I regret nothing about deciding to treat this particular client like the queen she is.

In life and in friendship, doing what's right can be just as rewarding as a huge commission.

But to be clear, it would be more rewarding with an Emmy.

///

SEVEN

Come and Knock on Our Door

L ong before Bravo, I was a boy realtor out there on my own, trying to rustle up clients any way I knew how. When you see how I live on the show now, it's easy to forget that I was new once too. Everyone begins from nothing, including me.

My favorite client was Somers's publicist Jay Bernstein. He was a big deal in his time, and he was everyone's publicist back in the sixties and seventies, singlehandedly changing the PR game in entertainment. Per the *Hollywood Reporter*, Bernstein "must have a direct line to God. When Jay starts talking, Hollywood listens."

I learned so much from him about making an impression. I'm a showman today because of what I witnessed by just being his friend. He pulled off stunts that no one had ever done before, like having *Entertainment Tonight*'s Mary Hart's legs insured for a million bucks apiece through Lloyd's of London. He was the mastermind behind paying ladies to toss their underpants and hotel room keys at an unsuspecting Tom Jones, forever cementing Jones as a sex symbol. Bernstein's the guy who took one look at Farrah Fawcett and realized the entire world would want to pin her poster to their bedroom walls; he made that happen.

But Bernstein was more than just a star-maker—he shined just as brightly due to his own merits. Back in the day, his underwater wedding was featured on *Lifestyles of the Rich and Famous*. He drove a big, convertible Rolls-Royce and wore Robert Evans glasses. To say he was a character is a profound understatement; the man was an icon.

I met him because his was the first door I ever knocked on; it was as easy as that. I'd just left my internship with Mentor and I was on my own, trying to get listings. For everyone who assumes I was handed my success, think again. I wasn't sitting around a brokerage, waiting for my parents' friends to list their homes with me, I was literally going door-to-door in Beverly Hills, like a Mormon on a mission. (Although imagine the confidence you'd feel if you thought Heavenly Father was directing you to interrupt someone's dinner. I had that confidence and more.)

Now, if you're reading this because you're considering a career in sales and your natural inclination isn't to talk to people? If you have no desire to form a connection? If the notion of knocking on doors makes you want to projectile vomit?

Yeah, you're going to fail.

If you're shy, we can work around that. Shyness isn't a permanent state. The key is remembering that everyone has a story, and most people are eager to share it. But if you're not naturally curious enough to find out what that story is, to make conversation and to share your story too, this isn't the job for you. Go build robots for a living. Maybe work in accounting.

Anyway, Jay and I spoke for a bit that first day. He was happy to talk to me, as his career had wound down and he was bored. I say this all the time: I am obsessed with an underdog. That day, he showed me all his Hollywood memorabilia. He gave me a tour of his house, including his trophy room from his big game hunts. He had gorillas, grizzly bears. You name it, he took his shot and his aim was impeccable. He was fearless.

Eventually, he and I ended up on his balcony, smoking cigarettes and chatting. He wasn't in the market to buy or sell, but I liked him; so when

I was door-knocking in his neighborhood, I'd always stop by because he appreciated having an audience. Ultimately, he had a story and I wanted to hear it.

A few years later, he passed away. Bernstein liked me, and his business manager respected the fact that we'd met by my knocking on his door, so I got the listing, and I sold his house.

———— /// ————

EIGHT

Get Your Mind on Your Marketing and Your Marketing on Your Mind

So much of my early career entailed me going from door to door, like an old-timey encyclopedia salesperson, before Wikipedia wiped this product off the map. Was it chic? No. But it was necessary. From working with Mentor, I was acquainted with how I should treat my clients, but I had to find them first. With my earliest buyers and sellers, it was easy to make them feel like my only client—because quite often, they were.

After I'd made my first sale and had a couple bucks in my pocket, I knew I needed to reinvest all that money into marketing. But how was I supposed to market listings I didn't yet have? And how could I insure I'd get listings for the kind of homes I hoped to represent?

That's why I did what anyone in my position would do—I chartered a helicopter to fly over all the neighborhoods and estates that I loved. These were the days before Google Earth, when an aerial photo was a rarity. I went up in the bird and photographed every one of the great old estates in Los Angeles. I love those properties the most, and they were the ones I wanted to sell. Like Babe Ruth, I was calling my shot.

I took hundreds and hundreds of photos, and once they were developed (this was before every phone had a camera), I had an outstanding excuse to knock on doors or otherwise be in contact. I took those four or five hundred pictures and reached out to every single one of those homeowners. I did this many times.

I'd give the photos to the homeowners as a gift, after explaining who I was and what I did (as to not appear like a crazed stalker). I'd explain that I thought they might like to have a photo of their spread.

To be clear, I never said, "Call me to sell your house," because that's pushy and inelegant, smacking of desperation and cheaply made shoes. Instead, I told them, "I'd love to send [or give, if I was in person] you a copy of this." And then they would get the photo, along with my card. If they wanted to call me back, great, and if they didn't want to call me, that was fine too. My goal was to get on their radar.

Guess what?

I sold *a lot* of houses this way.

Before those homeowners were ever my clients, I'd already proved to be an outside-the-box thinker who'd be creative in marketing their homes, so I was the natural choice. After all, I made it so easy with providing my contact info on the back of those shots.

The other thing I did with those photos was to create a database of every major estate on the Westside. Even though this was years ago, if I get a call for a listing today, there's a strong possibility that I'll come to their home prepared with a beautiful photograph, which never fails to impress the owner. The homeowner gets a memento of the house they're about to sell, and I get a listing. Everyone wins!

I'm never afraid to try something different when it comes to marketing, especially if it means a chopper ride. Another time, I took a client up to see properties in a helicopter—we even filmed this as an episode on the show. We landed it on a big piece of land that's now on the market for $300 million.

Okay, *technically*, we landed because I had to pee. Apparently *landing* is strictly forbidden in Beverly Hills, and we got a big, fat fine. But the whole thing was such a baller move that it was worth it. The client was so impressed by the lengths I'd go to sell him a house that he bought one of my listings.

FLAGG THIS

What are some outside-of-the-box actions you can take to differentiate yourself from your competition?

How could you best spend $100 on marketing? How about $1,000? Or $10,000?

Marketing is the surest way for a return on your investment, so it makes sense to funnel a portion of your earnings back into your business.

Here's the thing—you don't have to spend thousands of dollars to get in front of a potential client. In fact, the best $200 I ever spent was on an old book. I was antique shopping, and I ran across a leather-bound tome from 1942. It was full of old MLS listings from that time. I had all the pages laminated and then I sent them out to the houses that are still standing today. My note read, "Hi, I collect these sorts of things and thought you might appreciate owning a piece of history too."

Who's not going to say thank you for something as thoughtful as that?

Those thank-you notes started rolling in from these big estates, and I made friends with so many of the homeowners. What's funny is I've spent millions of dollars in marketing over the years yet ended up recouping almost all those costs with the listings that came from a $200 investment.

However, my tried-and-true method of marketing is sending mailers. I'm a huge proponent of using mailers to market to potential clients, twice a month like clockwork. If you're going to use print mailers as a realtor—and you should—the best and only way for you to see a return on this investment is to target the same homes again and again.

Redundancy is key.
Redundancy is key.
Redundancy is key.

What's the key? It's redundancy, no matter what you're selling. This is known as the rule of seven. Someone needs to see your ad seven times before they will act. In my experience, sometimes it's the rule of twenty-seven; not everyone is ready to sell their house when they see your ad. That doesn't mean you give up.

The temptation might be to spread these mailers around, hitting different neighborhoods at various times, casting a wide net. Let me ask you something—do you hate money? Do you want to set it on fire in a barrel in your backyard? No? Then don't make your aim scattershot. One mailer sent once to one new neighborhood is literally pissing into the wind . . . off the back of a helicopter. It's the repetition that gains the attention.

My mailers do one of two things—either get a homeowner to call me because after receipt of fifteen mailers, they're ready for me to sell their house. Or they call me to demand I cease and desist sending mailers, in which case I will charm the pants clean off them.

In the second case, if they ever do decide to sell, my persistence will be in the back of their minds.

———— *///* ————

NINE

Demented and Sad,
but Social

When I started in real estate, social media was in its nascent phase, so it's not something I needed to rely on in the beginning. After all, people have been buying and selling houses in some capacity since civilization moved off the forest floor and into well-lit caves with an open plan, close to transportation.

However, social media has become the great equalizer, allowing users to create their own content and level the playing field. You might not have an advertising budget, but if you're clever and creative, you can still reach millions. Per *Forbes*, 78 percent of salespeople who use social media outsell their peers, so it's to your benefit to figure out how to best incorporate it into your selling, TikTok dance optional.

Look at Dollar Shave Club, for example. They had a little-known razor subscription club. But with one viral video and some wisely placed Facebook ads, they blew up so much, they were eventually purchased by Unilever for $1 billion cash money, honey.

To be clear, their success didn't happen in a vacuum. The company was backed by venture capital firms, which helped fund their expansion. But if they hadn't had a quality product or the infrastructure in place to support the business social media brought in, they might have failed.

So social media should be part of your strategy but not necessarily your whole plan.

My social media presence is a lot like my career as a broker—a seamless blend of sales and social life. Every post or video is a considered decision, meant to either reinforce my brand or solicit feedback so I can tailor future interaction.

I use different platforms for different types of content, although there's plenty of cross-pollination. For instance, I post irreverent videos and in-depth celebrity interviews on my YouTube channel. While those are generally less real-estate focused and more fun, they drive interaction between all my social media presences and to my professional website.

I'm a visual person, so Instagram's my favorite and most frequent choice, and it's a catchall for everything I do. Now if I'm on a fabulous vacation, I'll use Instagram to intersperse the travelogue with new listings back home. You never have to scroll too far in my feed to be reminded that I sell homes for a living.

Facebook is an effective way to foster interaction and assess demographic information, while TikTok is pure fun, and it keeps me connected with my younger fans. Twitter is my go-to platform to post links to all the above.

While it's not important which platform you use, the key is to make sure you're using—and reaping the benefits—of at least one.

FLAGG THIS

What is your social media strategy? (If you don't have one, it's okay if you pledge *right now* to create one. If you're old enough to have school-aged kids, they can help.)

How can you incorporate the different platforms to enhance your pitch?

In what ways do you target potential customers through social media? Do you follow and contribute to specific groups? If not, join or create some.

Examine your own presence and consider either scaling back your subjective opinions or making that page private—you don't want to lose potential buyers because you're passionate about your feelings on, say, Representatives Marjorie Taylor Greene or Alexandria Ocasio-Cortez, or God forbid, CrossFit.

Spend an afternoon on TikTok or Instagram Reels to see how others are building brand awareness and attracting customers—you'll be surprised by the depth and breadth of what quick videos can make palatable and fun, up to and including dentistry and gynecology. Who knew?

———— /// ————

TEN

Who's on Your Hit List?

Realtors joke about the big three greatest drivers that cause sellers to list their homes—the Three Ds, if you will. They are disparity, divorce, and death. (Listen, I didn't say it wasn't a dark joke.) There are agents who specialize in liquidating distressed properties and those who are best known for helping divorcees start their second chapter in life. These brokers are most likely women of a certain age, Oscar Blandi blond, with sleeveless dresses highlighting arms that are as toned and strong as twisted steel cable.

Me? Give me death any day. Wait, that sounds ghoulish.

Let me explain—my favorite homes are the older estates in Beverly Hills. Nothing thrills me more than a property that hasn't been touched since President Johnson's administration. I delight every time I walk into what feels like a Slim Aarons photograph. Plus, there's an excellent chance that the person who's passed did so after a fabulous, long life; so selling the home is a big help to the family.

Does that mean I roam the halls of Cedars-Sinai like some slimy ambulance-chasing attorney? Of course not. Not chic. But do I keep track of the "goings" of Beverly Hill's most glamorous and prominent elderly residents through a variety of proprietary means? Let's just say, if someone over seventy crosses over the rainbow bridge in this town? I know first, and I have just the suit for it.

Now, there's a way to get these listings and not come across as a grief vulture. For instance, never call the family of the deceased when the body's not yet cold and say, "Hey, I hear your mom's dead. Wanna sell her house?" While there's no scientific method here, the wrong approach is to phone them the day after their beloved relative died, even if you send flowers and a card.

(Ask me how I learned this.)

Death is the most delicate situation I encounter as a broker, but often the most lucrative. Like so much in real estate, courting this business is a dance. I don't want to cut in too soon, as I'll look aggressive, and I don't want to wait too long, as the seller will likely find a different agent.

Two and a half weeks seems to be the sweet spot between grief subsiding and greed rising.

When I call, I introduce myself first and I wait a beat. There's a 60:40 chance they know me. It's easier if they do, but not necessary. If they don't recognize the name, I'll explain how I'm a Beverly Hills broker. This implies I'm not some unctuous bastard from Torrance who read the obit and saw dollar signs. (I feel like all his suits won't cost as much as my one.)

I'll highlight any connections we might have—maybe their beloved Gammy was a country club member with my grandparents, perhaps they served on a charitable board with my dad. As half my friend group comprises senior citizens, chances are good we've run in the same circles. What's important is they know I'm not a rando on a bus bench with his photo leering at passing cars. (There is nothing that says high-end realtor less than a shopping cart at Safeway.)

Then I will explain that I don't know what the family wants to do with the estate and that I'm not trying to get a listing today.

(Spoiler alert: I am *absolutely* trying to get a listing today.)

Instead, I'm calling to let the family know that I'm happy to be a resource for them. I'll say that they should have my number as I have a client who may be interested and that I'd love to peek at the place, if I could arrange that with their agent. This is an elegant way of asking, "Do you have an agent?" without asking.

More often than not, the family does not have an agent, and I'm able to meet them. If I can get in front of the family, I'm most likely to get the listing.

My approach is all about coming at the bereaved as someone who wants to help, because that is true. While working with them will benefit me, it will benefit the family more. I have the contacts, I have the expertise, I have the vision. They need me more than I need them, and that's exactly why I've been able get so many estate listings.

While landing the families' listings require far more finesse than if I were to pursue the other two Ds, I believe it's easier than trying to pump up my biceps.

—— /// ——

ELEVEN

Prequalify Your Clients

I was so eager to sell when I started my career, I'd take any- and every-one on as a client. I made the cardinal error of assuming if people wanted to look at houses, they had the finances to buy what we saw.

After wasting more than one Saturday on "real estate tourists," I learned to qualify a buyer before investing a second of my time. While I prefer to do business with previous clients or personal referrals (or the deceased), that's not always possible. In those cases, call me Nancy Drew because I'm about to investigate.

I had one potential buyer who seemed too good to be true. The gen-tleman came out of nowhere and wanted to spend millions of dollars. When I couldn't verify who he was on Google, I got creative. The po-tential client had mentioned a favorite hotel in London, so I called and dropped his name, saying I was considering a stay there based on his recommendations. The clerk was excited and shared that the man in question was a frequent guest, and he preferred the presidential suite. Yes! How do you like me now, Hardy Boys?

Until I determine a buyer can pay for what they see, I don't waste my precious time. Even once I've determined someone is solvent enough to buy from me, I verify that person is the decision maker. This is especially important outside the real estate realm. Don't be suckered into six months of white-tablecloth lunches, courting a gourmand middle man-ager who doesn't have the authority to sign a deal.

My advice is that you be discerning in who you pitch to, even if they are qualified to buy. Another time years ago, I started working with a nonagenarian. As the kids say, he was rich AF. We spent six months touring luxury home after home, but he never made an offer. I couldn't understand why. He had the means and wherewithal. Finally, my paternal grandmother, Edith, pointed out the obvious, telling me, "At ninety years old, it does not matter how much money you have. The only place you are moving to is the cemetery."

I guess the (non)buyer was looking for a bit of a last hurrah and some pleasant company. While he said he was interested, the truth was, he wasn't about to pack up sixty years of his life to move to greener pastures, and it took Edith to set me straight.

The lesson I took from this experience was to qualify each prospect not only financially but also mentally and emotionally. Just because they can buy doesn't mean they will. Now I invest my energy only on those who are serious about moving.

The flip side of this is to not be so discerning that I write off a potential client. Not long ago, I worked with someone who was looking to lease out their home. While this prospect sounds low rent (sorry, couldn't help myself), the simple fact is that leases can often turn to sales. Leases can take as much effort as a sale, but they shouldn't be dismissed out of hand, especially if you're an agent looking to build your business. Maybe this is how I get in the door (again with the puns, my apologies) with a homeowner.

In this example, my client owned a home on North Alpine. I helped them find quality renters for a small fee. After five years of appreciating the service I provided, they listed that rental home for sale through me.

I'd earned less than $10,000 on the rental, but my willingness to do the work made it possible for me to be first in line for their $13 million sale. And since my buyer bought the home, I was compensated on that end too.

That initial investment of my time turned into a $26 million sale and $500,000 in commissions.

So, when you treat your clients like every one of them represents a million-dollar account, don't be surprised when it becomes one.

———— /// ————

TWELVE

The Art of the Steal

I see many brokers who don't treat their clients properly, and it makes me twitchy. The natural inclination would be to swoop in and take them, but unlike in other industries where this is de rigueur, poaching clients is a big no-no in real estate.

That said, there are situations when clients come up for grabs because a listing contract expired or a seller-broker relationship has devolved. Brokers don't want to look desperate, sailing in the second the seller's first agent relationship hits the skids, like some gross dude trolling for newly single women outside divorce court. The lack of finesse in approaching someone else's former client is the fastest way to get branded a shitball in this business.

That said, it happens. All brokers are guilty of going after now-available clients because they need someone to sell their homes to, and we want to sell them. Our relationship is symbiotic.

For me, I'm not going to tarnish my reputation with a hard-sale blitz of phone calls to that seller, no matter how palatial the estate. Instead, I'm subtle. I work my sources—for example, I see whom we're both connected to on Facebook, and I'll aim for a personal recommendation. If *they* call *me*, it can't be considered poaching, right? A little trick of mine is, I call the title company and find out the names of everyone with a house for sale. I then have my assistant type every one of those names into Facebook and see mutual friends in common. Then, I offer the friend a referral fee or ask them to put us in touch, just to be nice. (This is one of my best ideas, if you ask me.) Another trick I have is whenever I get a monthly report of houses that have sold, I look up all the names of buyers and have title company check to see what other properties they own. Often, those people have homes they haven't sold yet.

If I know the seller, I'll find a way to bump into them at mutual haunts, such as a country club. If I can get in front of the seller and determine their home to be saleable, I can make them mine.

The key is finesse, and when executed with elegance, it's like the poaching never even happened. Honestly, Josh Altman is most like me in my approach, as he's the shrewdest of the *MDLLA* cast. Conversely, the less finesse one has in these situations, the worse that broker's reputation is.

Fortunately, I haven't been screwed over lately by other brokers poaching my people, for two reasons. First, my client base is largely left alone because I wouldn't take a listing I didn't love and wouldn't actively sell.

Second, I do everything in my power to make sure their homes are on the market at realistic prices. I never play the game of giving the highest number, therefore I'm not often in danger of losing them because the property isn't moving.

The bottom line is, other brokers can't poach my client when I've already sold their home.

FLAGG THIS

How do you retain your current client base? What steps can you take to ensure their loyalty?

Taking pricing out of the equation, why would your competitors' clients be better off working with you? How would you pitch them to steal that business?

---///---

THIRTEEN

Maintaining Client Relationships in Transactional Sales

Maintaining the intensity of a relationship with a buyer post-sale can be difficult because I can't be best friends with every single person to whom I've sold a house. It's hard because I get so close to them during the buying process. I have a front row seat to their hopes and dreams, as well as their fears and insecurities. Sounds like opening verse of a poem, yes? It's an emotional time, one that creates a hard and fast bond. I'm their sounding board. In many ways, I become their therapist.

What's tricky is after the sale closes: it's almost like I must break up with them. Ours is often a transactional relationship, as they have only one home to buy or sell and then they might be done for the next twenty years. There's no reason for us to be in touch all day, every day. I send Christmas cards and the occasional text message, but it's not the same. Once a year, I do look through all my contacts and send quick hello texts so they know I at least think of these clients from time to time.

Consider this—I have so many clients, but to them, I'm the only person they have. They have one broker; I have a thousand clients. So when I'm not a constant in their lives post-sale, it can be hurtful. That's why I do what I can to ease the transition.

Back when COVID was becoming real and no one knew what would happen next, I sent all my previous clients liquor-filled candies and a note that essentially said, "In these uncertain times, the only things we can count on are chocolates and booze."

Who'd have guessed the housing market would explode during a global pandemic? I was busier than ever, and a lot of my business came from clients who received those boxes. Speaking of the pandemic, what made someone wake up one day in the middle of a global health crisis and say to themselves, "Let's start buying real estate!" It's totally counter-intuitive, but you don't see me complaining! But I'm sure several condo owners are. No one wants to be trapped in an elevator with someone sneezing. It used to be that you coughed to cover up a fart, but since COVID, you fart to cover up a cough. (You like that one, eh? I'm pretty funny if I say so myself. And speaking of, I wasn't as careful as I should have been after getting vaxxed. I went around practically licking door-knobs and nothing happened. So, either science is real or even the disease doesn't want me.)

My point is, it's worth it to keep the lines of communication open post sale, because I'll tell you what—all those families who wanted their forever homes to have an open floor plan? The people whom I didn't think I'd see again until their kindergartner went off to college? When the pandemic hit, suddenly everyone desired homes with separate live/work areas, filled with solid walls and doors that lock. Yeah, the pandemic was great for real estate people. But my dad was pissed because his office buildings seemed to be harder to fill in those days.

Anyway, because you never know, keep in touch.

—————— /// ——————

FOURTEEN

The Converse Is Don't Let Them Buy Trash

A critical part of establishing trust with my clients is for them to not feel like I'm selling to them. But to be clear, my job *is* selling, so it's a balancing act. I'm out there showing homes every day with every intention of getting paid for people having purchased them; I'm not about being anyone's tour guide. (It's like the Girlfriend Experience, only for houses.) If I wanted to be a docent, I'd just hang around historic Greystone Mansion waiting for unsuspecting German tourists to wander past.

The easiest way for me to demonstrate to my clients that I'm on their side is to bring them to a property that has aspects they might like but I know isn't ideal. Maybe it's too far from work, perhaps it's too close to a busy street, or there's not enough square footage. Possibly it's just too early in the sales process and they don't even know what they like yet. The key is there's enough upside to the property to pique their interest: say, it's styled nicely or comes in below their budget.

I must establish a listing they like right up front so that I can kill it. I can be super dramatic about it too, all, clutching my pearls and shouting, "This house is horrible! Hell, no!"

Sometimes I'll use silence as a strategy, depending on my buyers' personalities. When I don't say anything, my buyers will pick up on my quiet dislike, offering up what they think I might believe is wrong with the home, thus talking themselves out of it.

This strategy accomplishes two things—first, it demonstrates that I'm not greedy (well . . .) and prone to shoehorn them into any old place that sticks (truth), and second, that I'm their advocate (also truth).

Essentially, I'm the blunt friend who'll tell them their ass looks huge in those pants, when everyone else is protecting their feelings because they're afraid of conflict and hurt feelings. Clients expect me to agree when they're into a home's vibe, and when I don't, it's jarring, but in an effective way.

So the flip side of the "don't sell garbage" coin is that I won't let my buyers buy trash. (Mind you, I try to show them only places that are at my taste level, so the idea of trash is relative.)

Quite often, I know the exact home my buyers should purchase, but I must guide them to this decision, and being sales-y is the surest way to raise their hackles and scare them away.

When my clients see that I'll fight them on a bad home, they can be confident in my enthusiasm when I bring them to the right one.

I'll take my check now, please.

//////

FIFTEEN

The Salesman's Psychology

Why have I been so successful in closing deals?

Sparkling wit and sartorial panache aside, of course.

The answer is counterintuitive—I'm successful because I don't push. I wouldn't wheedle. I'd never pressure. Everything I do is client-centric.

I approach each potential sale with the client's best interests at heart, so I don't need to rely on amateur tactics paired with an assumptive close. I would rather bunk at the Red Roof Inn than ask a buyer, "So we've agreed this is the perfect place for you—what would it take to get you into this house today?"

Ugh. So gross. I can't.

While I use the terms "salesperson" and "dealmaker" interchangeably in this book, I must mention there's a slight difference in the taxonomy. All dealmakers are salespeople, but not all salespeople are dealmakers.

Confused? Allow me to explain.

A salesperson's job is to sell—to get the potential client to buy the pants, sign the service contract, ink the deal. In this scenario, any tactics are acceptable provided the sale gets closed. There's no tacit understanding between the buyer and seller that these are the most flattering trousers, that the service contract is their most prudent option, or that the deal benefits both parties and not just the person collecting the commission. And if there's buyer's remorse afterward? That's not the seller's problem.

Even though "salesman" is a semantic shortcut to explain my job, the difference is, I'm a *dealmaker.* The buyer's satisfaction is at the top of mind in every deal, and of the same import.

FLAGG THIS

The art of the deal now means that both parties must equally benefit from the sale.

The days of real estate moguls crushing the competition and bullying buyers into one-sided agreements are over—you're fired!

The professional dealmaker understands a buyer's psychology. The minute my client thinks I'm trying to pressure them into writing an offer for just anything, their defenses go up and I lose all credibility as a trusted advisor.

So, how does one make the leap from sales closing to dealmaking?

First, it's critical to have an opinion. Amateurs are the ones running around saying yes to everything the client likes, instead of lending value by offering an informed opinion. Most salespeople would rather the client like them than potentially screw up the sale by sharing a contrary opinion. I do not suffer from this affliction.

Buyers assume that whomever they're working with has the depth of knowledge about the service or product. Unfortunately, some salespeople know everything about pressuring a buyer into signing *right now* and nothing about the marketplace for what they're selling. They taint the reputations of all of us who make deals for a living.

In the case of realtors, we brokers should be educating our clients based on our familiarity with the marketplace. But so many in my field would rather just sign a deal than level with their clients on why they shouldn't like a bad house. What they refuse to realize is exactly how much credibility and trust honesty builds. They'll never push a buyer off a property they don't like because they lack the confidence in themselves to speak up; they're too afraid to lose the potential sale.

But when a buyer trusts us, they will buy from us, whether it's this house today or the better house we'll show them next week.

In a related point, it's impossible to make the leap from sales to deal-making if that seller can't learn to speak up. There are times my client loves a house that I don't. In cases like this, I explain that they hired me for my expertise, and I would be remiss if I didn't share it. I'll never rip apart the house; instead, I focus on the facts that have influenced my opinion. I'm not the decision maker, and if they are dying for the house I don't like, that's certainly their right. I just want them to have all the information before they make their decision. Again, this builds trust and credibility.

Dealmakers are the people who always have their clients' best interests at heart. For example, let's say I have clients who have fallen in love with a brand-new home located in an undesirable area. The family wants to write an offer. A salesperson wouldn't think twice about closing the deal and cashing that check. What's the downside, right? The buyers loved and wanted that home . . . at least, until they move in and discover the park view they so admired is now marred by the bars they had to put on their windows.

As a dealmaker, I won't allow my client to make an unwise investment without a fight. I'll explain what's wrong with the poorly located property, and I'll try to find them an even better home in a more desirable location.

Keep in mind, a salesperson wants a one-off sale.

A dealmaker facilitates a long-term relationship with a repeat buyer.

In my case, this happens when I demonstrate to my clients that I'm protecting them from the aforementioned bad investment. When I try to talk buyers out of wasting their money and into listening to me, I say, "This is a lot like going to an $800/hour criminal attorney and then not heeding their recommendations. (If you want to get to death row, this is the easiest way to go to it.) While ultimately you make your own decisions, you're paying me a big chunk of change for my advice and experience, so I'm giving it to you."

The few times buyers haven't accepted my advice, they came back later, telling me I was right and asking me to help them make a better decision now. (And P.S., could I find a buyer for a lovely home with new steel window bars and Crazy Riders gang–adjacent?)

In real estate, a good broker is a guide, a facilitator. Part of being a dealmaker and not just a salesperson is the depth and breadth of knowledge we bring to the deal. My dealmaker peers and I can tell you how much every single home on a block sold for, how much debt is on the house, when the house last sold before this sale, and basically everything else about the property, save for the color of the new homeowner's underpants. (Probably pink, in my experience.)

A salesperson will know only the reasons why you should sign a deal right now and here's a pen.

So, ask yourself, are you a salesperson or a dealmaker?

And if you came up with salesperson, do you want to be a dealmaker?

Because the million-dollar mindset favors the latter, and your clients will thank you for it.

///

SIXTEEN

Sell to the Man in Sweatpants

I love eccentric clients the most—they're so much more interesting than normies. I imagine this comes from growing up around Edith.

In the nascent days of my career, a gentleman named Hank called me about a property that I'd just sold. I told him that place was no longer available but I could show him other homes.

When Hank pulled up, he was dressed in tattered clothing and driving a twenty-five-year-old Mercedes. Edith always taught me to beware of the guy with the Rolex and the Bentley and that it's the guy in sweatpants you want as your customer.

In retrospect, I suspect Edith was projecting. (Unlike Edith, not every homeless-looking woman carries a bankroll and twelve Krugerrands in her brassiere. Sometimes, it's just a bag of bottlecaps and cigarette butts.) While I'd eventually be burned by not prequalifying my buyers, in this instance, her advice was still top of mind, especially because Hank was only my second client; what did I have to lose?

The first time we went out to look at houses, Hank took me to eat at Mr. Chow's, and we got on like a house on fire. Again, I love eccentric. Give me Little Edie Bouvier Beale and a baby raccoon in her Birkin over a Wall Street bro any day of the week.

Anyway, Hank and I fell into a pattern—he'd pick me up in his beat-up Benz, wearing his usual uniform of sweatpants. Then he'd take me somewhere magnificent for lunch (his treat), ordering ten different things so we could taste them all. Of course, he'd end up with half of the dishes splattered on his pants as he had a propensity for spilling. Then we'd spend the afternoon seeing homes he liked but didn't love.

Other brokers found out I was working with Hank, and they thought I was an idiot. They'd tell me, "Hank's broke. He looks but never buys. He's just wasting your time." But here's the thing—I've been around moneyed people my whole life. I can sniff out wealth like a truffle pig. I didn't care that Hank lived in a shoebox in the unfashionable part of Beverly Hills. And I was charmed that he dressed off the Goodwill racks. While all signs pointed otherwise, I felt in my gut he was authentic.

Hank persuaded me to join his walking club, where he and his old cronies would stroll Armand Hammer Park every afternoon and discuss real estate. As I'd walk and talk with the group, I discovered we had several people in common, and every one of them backed up my suspicion—Hank wasn't broke, he was just unpretentious and oddly selective about real estate. It's not that he wasn't buying because he couldn't; he wasn't buying because he hadn't seen the perfect property yet.

Or *maybe* no one treated him like he was their only client.

The more I walked with the group, the more I could picture Hank's ideal home. But it wasn't on the market. Yet.

I had an idea.

I called one of my attorneys and said, "Ted, I'd like to show your house to my client. Would you consider selling it if I could get you around $10 million?"

Ted replied, "Josh, for that for that much money, I would sell you my wife." (Mind you, $10 million back then was like $25 million today.)

I took Hank to Ted's Bel Air home, and I was right—it was exactly what Hank wanted. He purchased the place for $9 million cash, and we closed in a week. (Ted's wife did not convey, possibly because he didn't get the full ask.)

Of course, the week after the deal closed, Hank completely razed Ted's home, even though it was a designer showplace with top-of-the-line finishes.

I'm telling you, *eccentric.*

So, Edith was right, and I'd made my second sale. I earned not only a hefty commission but also bragging rights over the brokers who doubted me. Win-win.

Did I eventually alienate some of these same brokers with my arrogance and gloating over my growing string of wise decisions?

Yes. But that's a story for another chapter.

/ / /

SEVENTEEN

The Personal Touch

One of the smartest moves you can make as a dealmaker is to increase your social circle; for me, the more people I know, the more potential clients I have. As a social animal, it's my nature to make friends, so this is just an added benefit to being a dealmaker. I love talking to new people! Sometimes I drive my friends and family crazy when we're out together and I spend so much time chatting with everyone around us. There's never a stranger when I'm nearby.

Cultivating relationships is not only pleasant and entertaining, but it's a sure way to enhance your business. I do favors for friends all the time, and they react in kind. When I first started out, I considered every broker my competition/mortal enemy, so it didn't occur to me that we could not only enjoy each other's company but also be a sounding board for one another. I wasn't yet secure enough in my position to trust anyone else.

Because of the relationships I've since fostered, I have a myriad of folks I can rely on to have my back, and I have theirs too. I can dole out assistance to or call it in from people everywhere, anywhere from the Recorder of Deeds office to the US Marshals to the front desk at the Beverly Wilshire.

In *The Tipping Point*, Malcolm Gladwell (I know, I know, enough with this guy; yes, clearly, I'm a fan) talks about the three types of people in relation to the spread of ideas—connectors, mavens, and salespeople. You'd assume I'd be a salesperson, as they're characterized as larger than life, always wanting to be the center of attention. While those are some of my (best) traits, at my core, I'm honestly more of a connector.

Per Gladwell, connectors like me are "people who link us up with the world. People with a special gift for bringing the world together," because we cultivate networks of friends. He explains, "The point about connectors is that by having a foot in so many different worlds, they have the effect of bringing them all together."

Even if you're a sole practitioner in your position, I guarantee you'll do more in your job when a few friends have your back.

When I treat my buyers like my friends (because they so often are, especially when we're in the thick of things), it cultivates such a personal touch in all our dealings. One of the most important practices I learned from working with Mentor was how to do business with said individualized touch because people love and remember that kind of thing.

For example, Mentor didn't work out of an impersonal real estate office—he conducted most of his business from his home, and it was so elegant and WASPy. If he had a closing, he'd have all parties come to his house and they'd sign paperwork by his pool while he served drinks—it was Golden Age of Hollywood elegance.

My favorite place for a meeting or a closing is in my emerald green dining room. I have a giant jade-colored table that seats twenty I inherited from Edith. The room is spare and dramatic, lit by a 1960s Venini chandelier and a couple Billy Haines parrot lamps once gifted to Betsy Bloomingdale from President and Nancy Reagan. The emerald green buffet features a pair of Murano glass panthers and a perpetual motion Jaeger-LeCoultre Atmos gold clock, which functions by changes in temperature. I use beautiful Herend china and gorgeous St. Louis crystal, with a chef-prepared lunch showcasing stone crabs (when in season). It's retro and chic, and what better way to communicate to a buyer or seller that they worked with the right broker? To give the room a modern twist, the room features four Norman Seeff photographs of Cher, Steve Jobs, Ray Charles, and Tina Turner. The dining room always has fresh flowers, generally white roses leaning out of large white vases in homage to Jeff Leathem and the George V in Paris.

People default to remembering their last interaction with a salesperson, and what a way to make a final impression! The subliminal message is, *Here's the life I've created by taking care of my clients; you made the right choice.* And wouldn't you feel better about paying $10 million for a home during the closing paperwork at a private, catered event, rather than, say, a Panera? And just think about the twenty bucks you saved on valet parking.

Also, what's a Panera?

––––––– /// –––––––

EIGHTEEN

A Convenient Woman

When I'm asked about my favorite client or deal, I never hesitate when I give the answer—it's the Betsy Bloomingdale estate.

I met Betsy Bloomingdale the first time on a Sunday afternoon. Bloomingdale was a socialite and philanthropist, but neither of those terms adequately describe the force of nature she was. She'd married the heir to the Bloomingdale's department store chain and served in the unofficial capacity as the "First Friend" to President Ronald and Nancy Reagan. Betsy wasn't a fixture of Los Angeles society so much as she *was* Los Angeles society, her social graces eclipsed only by her generosity. People referred to her as "Good Queen Betts" for a reason.

So, as I waited on the doorstep of her Holmby Hills estate before meeting her for the first time, I had every confidence that she'd be fabulous.

The full extent of her charisma wasn't evident until she swung open the ornately carved double doors. Because it was a lazy Sunday afternoon, I couldn't expect her full-court fashion press that had been making the news since she first hit *Vanity Fair*'s Best Dressed List five decades previously. Plus, she was in her nineties; arthritis is real, and buttons can be a bitch for the best of us. After all, she'd made her sartorial statement millions of times previously, and maybe the drive to be so glamorous had run its course. While I didn't anticipate yoga pants (can you even imagine?), I figured she'd retired the kind of couture she wore at her parties, where she'd hosted everyone from Henry Kissinger to Michael Jackson.

Here's the thing—I'm narcissistic enough to not be impressed by most people. I can't build a potential client's confidence by fan-boying all over him or her; I need to be viewed as an equal. And given whom I come from, I've been a part of LA's society since birth, too. Betsy wasn't even going to be the first icon I met that week, so I wasn't beside myself with nerves.

When I meet important or famous people, it's imperative they understand I speak their language and I run in their circles. Because of this habit, I've become friends with icons you wouldn't believe specifically because no one else has the confidence to speak to them like they're real people with feelings and frailties and shitty taste in TV shows.

But then I met Queen Betts.

The doors opened and Betsy appeared just as a maharani. She opened the door in a flowing ball gown, cutting an imperious yet welcoming figure, her eyes twinkling and her signature smile on full display. I felt like I'd stumbled into an issue of *Women's Wear Daily*. She was decked out in handfuls of diamonds and rubies. Literally—handfuls. In her throaty voice, she said, "Hello, dawllllinngggg. Would you care for cocktails on the veranda? We're having mint juleps!" Behind her, the scent of heirloom roses and Chanel No. 5 wafted from the sun-drenched entrance hall where I spied an Iberian mahogany settee.

Truth? I went weak in the knees. In that moment, I had to ask myself, "Am I suddenly straight?" The second question I asked myself was, "How come I don't have a veranda?"

I was not worthy. Still, I pulled myself together and stepped inside the Promised Land of her nine-bedroom (and eleven-closet) Italianate villa. Her home was a living time capsule from a more elegant yesteryear. This must have been how Charlie felt when walking into Willy Wonka's chocolate factory, except I wasn't going to try to taste all the surfaces. Yet.

Betsy's home had been meticulously decorated by the iconic designer Billy Haines in a Hollywood Regency aesthetic. Born William Haines, Billy had once been a Hollywood leading man and an enormous box office draw, but he'd lost his contract with MGM after refusing to break up with his partner Jimmie Shields.

Did he apologize for being who he was? No.

Did he curl up and die over what he lost? No.

Instead, he pivoted to interior design where his work became synonymous with glamour and luxury. His legacy is far beyond what he might have achieved as an actor. Naturally, Haines is my favorite designer, and I love that he rarely signed his work as he believed that the design should speak for itself. As I explained in an interview with *House Beautiful*, "Most of the estates that Billy Haines designed have been dismantled or sold off, so there really are no complete houses left that were fully designed by [him]." I was borderline giddy as I toured that dream come to life.

We breezed through rooms bathed in golden light from the open-air atrium, admiring the hand painted chinoiserie wallpaper and botanical prints. As we passed low-slung leather veneered chairs and gondola sofas, I felt breathless picturing decades of famous women arranging their skirts on those famous "hostess chairs" pieces while having important conversations with maharajas and heads of state.

Again, I asked myself, "Is my sexual orientation suddenly for nonagenarians?"

Although she impressed so much upon me, Betsy became my spirit animal when it comes to elegant entertaining. That afternoon, she explained to me how she always included a few of those who she deemed "marvelously wacky" guests—often artists or professors—because she didn't want her parties to be boring.

We bonded over conversations about art and politics and travel. I was rapt as she detailed the true roots of style, which have nothing to do with money and everything to do with knowledge and experience.

I was smitten. I may or may not have proposed on the spot.

After I confirmed she wasn't headed to Cougar Town in search of small, fey Jewish men (damn it), she shared her favorite entertaining tips. She told me about keeping a series of leather-bound books, each embossed with the title *Ma Table*, where she'd document every detail of her soirees, from seating arrangements to outfits, to make sure no one ever experienced the same party twice. I've since incorporated her tricks into my life. On her advice, I even bought a butler stick, which is a wooden tool that looks like a yardstick. Actually, it is a yardstick on one side, but on the other, it centers at 0" where the plate goes, and the measurements go outward by inch. That way all the flatware can be laid out in a mirror image because the symmetry of the setting is what makes it beautiful. (No, you can't just "eyeball" it, you savage.)

Thanks to Betsy's tutelage, I'm much more prone to having potential clients to my house for lunch rather than taking them out. It's one thing to tell luxury buyers that I embrace their taste levels—it's entirely another to demonstrate it in my own home, providing the kind of experience that makes my clients feel like they're the most important people I ever met.

My point is, I connected with Betsy Bloomingdale that first day. As we sipped our mint juleps (seriously, did I die and go to WASP heaven?), I expressed my appreciation and admiration for the impact she had on the world. She knew I cherished her home and felt fiercely protective of it; I wanted to preserve who and what she was forever. We were kindred spirits.

That's why when she passed in 2016, I was her family's natural choice of broker, and not just because I was close with her grandson and his wife.

I quietly put out word that the home was available, bypassing the usual practice of posting data and photos on the MLS. While my rule is to publicize everything, sometimes I must break the rules. At no point was the house advertised or listed publicly. I shuddered at the thought of some developer razing a piece of American history to erect a massive white box. Betsy would have hated that . . . and yet I would have welcomed her haunting me, so you can see my dilemma.

I didn't need to shout that this house was available, I only needed to whisper. I had every confidence the *right* buyer would purchase it in an off-market transaction, and that's exactly what happened. (Read *Variety* if you want to know the rest of the story, but to be clear, I wasn't the one who leaked the story to the press, regardless of what Tom Ford believes. I hate to break it to him, but the idea of jeopardizing my commission by outing the sale before it even closed escrow? Not in this lifetime. What really gets me is I *saved* this sale for Tom Ford. He's in this home because of me. The day before we closed escrow, I received an offer for $1 million *over* what Ford negotiated. I literally fought to allow him to buy the house, because a) Betsy would have wanted it that way, and b) I didn't need the gay mafia to cancel me. So maybe Ford should cool it with the vendetta so I don't have to scowl every time I drop $25,000 in his store for impeccably cut trousers.)

Now, this is the part where I'd tell you about how much commission I banked from selling this listing, except I used every penny I earned to buy up as much of the Bloomingdale's collection of Billy Haines pieces as I could.

So . . . yes. Apparently, I'm still gay.

But the point I want to impress upon you is that when you treat your clients like they're your only clients, they will respond in kind, and the lifestyle you want will be yours for the taking.

NINETEEN

No Easy Day

There's a good reason why I chose to document today for this book. The impetus for it began yesterday, and it's why I had an extra-hard time sleeping last night, because it's the possible culmination of everything I've ever worked toward and the only client I would literally die to land.

No pressure there.

I was in the middle of a meeting in my dining room yesterday when my phone rang. I frowned at it. I hate interruptions—they ruin the flow of the meeting. A handful of buyer agents paused in their discussion and looked at me, as did my assistant, Hilary. I raised my hand in apology.

"What?" I barked into the phone, tearing off a piece of bagel. Then I sighed. It was already stale.

Claire was on the line. "Josh, I'm sorry to interrupt. A woman named Anastasia Beaverhausen is on the line. Shall I take a message or tell her to call back after the meeting?"

The bagel turned to cement in my mouth. Anastasia Beaverhausen? *That* Anastasia Beaverhausen? (Obvi a pseudonym—sorry, I can't kiss and tell about this fabulously wealthy and fiercely private woman.)

No. It couldn't be. My heart pounded and my veins filled with ice.

The others started talking again and I realized I needed privacy, stat.

I dropped my piece of bagel and stood up. "Shut up! Transfer the call to my office. Now! Please! Oh, my God!"

Claire was unflappable, as per usual. "Sounds good."

I rushed down the hall, slamming my office door in my haste. Could this really be happening? Was I dreaming? I waited for the phone to ring, practically vibrating as I paced in tiny circles. What was taking so long?

My fingers drumming on the desk, the phone finally sounded. I closed my eyes and took a deep breath, trying to calm my nerves. I grabbed the trash can in case I needed to barf. Ugh. It was made of mesh. That wouldn't work at all.

I took a steadying breath before I answered.

"Josh here," I said, trying to project the confidence that I did not feel.

I'd spent four years envisioning what this woman looked like, what she sounded like. I'd even wondered what she might smell like. Tuberoses? Neroli? Krugerrands? I didn't know and I'd give anything to find out!

I didn't want to be my usual self and potentially scare her off, having tried for years to track this woman down, failing every time.

I had to play it cool.

"This is Anastasia Beaverhausen," the smoky voice on the other end of the line purred. She purred like Eartha Kitt! I had to stop myself from swooning. I opened my mouth but found my words would not come. For the first time in my life, the words wouldn't come. I was too eager, too nervous, and too frightened to not ask the question I'd so long ago swallowed down, along with a bite of that cement bagel.

Thankfully, after a few seconds, I found my voice and blurted out my question. "Please don't be offended by my question but do you know [that supericonic California billionaire whom I can't name]?"

Silence was my only answer.

Well, that and the sound of her exhaling. Three seconds ticked by, and I thought to myself, "Way to go, Josh. You couldn't stop yourself, could you? All you had to do was listen and wait to see if she revealed something. What if you scared her off? *WTF is wrong with you?*"

"Yes."

A lifetime passed in silence, although it was probably more like three seconds. What did I say next? I couldn't offer, "I've been waiting for this phone call for years," because she'd think I was a stalker for sure.

I told myself, "Breathe. Breathe. Breathe and say something, you idiot. How are you a multimillion-dollar negotiator when you can't even say boo?"

I cleared my throat and tried to find words. "Ms. Beaverhausen, how can I help you?"

Okay, good. Cool, cool, cool. Not psychotic sounding. Keep it up, you got this.

She said, "Well, the reason for my call is, I know you deal with a lot of historical homes, and I had a few questions regarding the porte cochere on my property."

What in the actual fuck was this woman talking about?

I was so thrown off by her question that I forgot to be nervous for a minute.

I listened as she went on. "I want to thank you, by the way, for the lovely advertisement you mailed regarding my home from the 1930s." (She pronounced advertisement the way only rich people do, like *ad-VER-tis-ment*.)

Also, what ad?

I began pawing at all the papers on the desk, as though I might find the answer there.

That's when it clicked.

About a year earlier, I sent an old photo advertisement to a home in East Gate Bel Air. I collect Beverly Hills real estate memorabilia, and I'd come across the old ad and thought the homeowner might appreciate it the way I did. It was just a little something to frame and put on the wall, a conversation piece, something for guests to admire. I figured the homeowner would get a kick out of seeing how the home had increased in value from the 1940s when it sold for $75,000, to today with a value of $7.5 to $8 million. (What did I tell you about L.A. real estate, right?)

She said she was considering doing some work to her porte cochere but didn't want to undertake any design that might break any rules regarding setbacks on her property. "The city is so funny these days about these things, you know?"

My mind raced. Should I continue to play it cool? Be like Fonzie? Or should I go in for the kill? I didn't want to scare her away, but this might be the only chance I'd have, considering every realtor worth his or her salt in all of southern California has been trying to have a conversation with this woman for thirty years.

Thirty freaking years.

Finally, I said, "Ms. Beaverhausen, I'm happy to answer any questions I can for you, but I have to say, I'm not sure how much help I can be. I was wondering if I might ask you something?"

"I am not going to sell my estate."

"No, no, no, it's nothing like that."

Her estate is arguably her most valuable property. My head was swimming with so many things, I couldn't even figure out what I wanted to ask her. What was wrong with me? Thank God I wasn't being filmed— I'd never live this down.

I tried to give myself a pep talk to get through the rest of this conversation. Don't blow it, Flagg. If you irritate her, or get too personal, you may never be able to get anything out of her.

Another steadying breath. "Okay. I've got this," I said to myself.

"Ms. Beaverhausen? I have been trying to track you down for years. Sorry, I know that sounds odd. I would hate to make you feel uncomfortable. But ever since I was a kid, I've been fascinated by real estate. In fact, when I turned sixteen, the first thing I did was hop in my car and drive down every single road in Bel Air, Beverly Hills, and the Bird Streets. Most kids would drive to their friend's houses but not me. I got the keys, and I was off to the races."

As the word vomit spews out, I was thinking to myself that if someone I called started telling me his or her life story after forty seconds, I would probably hang up and block their number.

I estimated I had about thirty more seconds to gain her interest and trust, to establish a rapport. I couldn't just ask her a bunch of personal questions about her properties. This is a woman who's never had her

photograph taken, never responded to anyone's letters or calls, and be-
fuddled all the real estate junkies for years. I couldn't just ask right out,
"Why in the world do you have $200 million in abandoned prime Los
Angeles real estate? Why are you holding some of L.A.'s trophy properties, and they sit there completely empty?"

No, that would definitely not work. Wrong tactic. I needed to butter
her up with my life story and my fascination for real estate. I had to
demonstrate to her that we were in the same tribe, simpatico, that we
spoke the same language.

It was imperative I set the tone for what I was dying to ask her. But I
couldn't just start bombarding her with questions like a firing squad,
tempting though it may be. "Ms. Beaverhausen, I can remember driving
those roads and stumbling across [fancy named estate] and wondering
what was on the other side of those massive gates of your estate."

The last time I drove past, it didn't appear to have been touched since
the Truman administration. I kept this fact from exiting my fat mouth,
instead, saying, "Ms. Beaverhausen, why is the house abandoned?"

I was sweating profusely, armpits damp, mouth a little dry. I was
going to want to towel off the desk chair by the time I was done here.

She got quiet again, the silence stretching for a few seconds. Shit, did
I offend her?

"Let me guess, you want to know about [fancy beach estate] in Malibu too?" Ms. Beaverhausen asked.

She was loosening up and talking my language. I didn't even need to
ask her about her Malibu Beach property—she brought it up herself. I
couldn't tell—was she pissed that I called her home abandoned or had I
hooked her?

"Well, to be honest, I'd like to know about the beach house, [another
estate], [estate], and [estate, which is a freaking lot of estates for those of
you keeping track]. Quite frankly, I'd like to know everything about
you. You're a mystery, Anastasia." Shit, did I just call her by her first
name? I stumbled to correct myself, "Sorry, I meant Ms. Beaverhausen."

"Anastasia is just fine."

I died. I did.

"Anastasia, have you ever heard of Huguette Clark?"

"No, who is he?"

"Um, *she*. Now, I may have you all wrong, Anastasia, but I think of you as somewhat of a Huguette Clark."

I took the silence from her as my cue to continue.

"She was the copper heir, daughter to Senator William A. Clark, Sr. He'd made his fortune in the railroads and copper mines and owned some of the greatest real estate in California and New York. Senator Clark owned a townhouse spanning a city block on New York City's Fifth Avenue. It would easily be worth $275 million if it were still in existence. He also owned a sprawling fourteen-acre estate in Connecticut and, quite arguably, one of the most valuable properties in all of California, Bellosguardo, a twenty-acre promontory on the bluffs above the Pacific Ocean in the Montecito section of Santa Barbara, California."

Hello? Hello?! I didn't want to ask if she was still there, or if I was giving a history lesson to myself. Still, I continued with tales of Ms. Clark's eccentricities. After ten minutes of talking, I realized she hadn't said anything in quite some time. Did she hang up? Should I ask if she's still there? Was I speaking English? *What's the frequency, Kenneth?*

"Well, that truly does sound like a remarkable story, Josh. I'd like to hear more about it."

I wanted to dance around the office, crowing, "And *that's* why it's important to know your shit!" But I refrained.

"I'll send you a copy of *Empty Mansions*. Ana? Can I call you that? Would you like to get a drink?"

"Oh, well, I'm really not that social."

No. I *needed* to meet her.

"Ana," wait, so I was definitely calling her *Ana* now? "It would be the greatest honor to just sit down with you and pick your brain. I'm not looking for a listing. I know they're not for sale." I didn't give her a chance to say no, instead asking, "How about tomorrow early evening? Can I take you to the Polo Lounge at 6:30?"

"Where is that?" Not really the response I'm expecting from the mistress of the son of one of the wealthiest men in the world.

"Oh, it's at the Beverly Hills Hotel."

"Never been."

I was losing her. I could feel it. I tried another location. "Well, how about the Hotel Bel Air?"

"I haven't been there in years."

"Well, now's as good of a time as any! So how about it?"

The phone was silent, the seconds ticking away. "Well, I guess it couldn't hurt."

Do you believe in miracles?!

"Can I pick you up?" I slapped my palm to my forehead, and it made a damp smacking sound, sure to leave a mark. What a stupid question. Why would she want to get into a car with a complete stranger?

She was quick to answer. "No."

I didn't push my luck. When you have the sale, stop selling!

Before she changed her mind, I said, "Well, okay, see you tomorrow at 6:30!"

I hung up and just sat, staring at the phone. I did it. I actually did it. I arranged a face-to-face meeting with Anastasia Freaking Beaverhausen!

"Okay," I said to myself. "Now, I have to tell everyone."

I called some friends to brag about my accomplishment. They didn't believe me, as this coup was akin to having Santa Claus or Hanukkah Harry or the Easter Bunny call me, but I didn't care. I knew she was real, and that was all that mattered.

I was riding high on scoring the meeting with Anastasia when I received a cryptic text. It came through from a number I didn't recognize. It said, "Nice talking Josh; I think it's probably best we don't meet."

"Fuckkkkkkk!" I yelled.

Right away, I responded, "Ana, I was so excited to meet you. I really hope you can make it. I promise I don't want anything from you. I just want to chat."

An hour went by with no response, and I began to wonder if I'd hear from her again. Would *I* show up if I were in her shoes? Hell, no. I'd be afraid someone wanted to make my skin into a suit, a la Buffalo Bill.

Was it even real, or was the call somehow an elaborate dream sequence?

She finally sent a simple reply. "Okay," and all was right in my world again.

I replied to her message. "See you tomorrow." I refrained from expressing myself in a nonsensical string of emojis. So that's what's on deck for this evening. Because I'm a pro, I'll not only get through my day before our dinner tonight, but I'm going to give my all to my clients, like I do every day.

If I don't throw up first.

PART THREE

———— /// ————

Up Your Attitude

The truth is, no matter how good you are at something in life, you always need to push yourself past your limits. If you expect to get small clients, you'll get small clients. Confidence is something your buyer can sniff out from a mile away. How can you expect someone you work with to trust you with their sale if you don't trust your own abilities?

TWENTY

///

Confidence Begins with a C and Ends with You

The key to understanding my attitude is that I am never not selling an image and a lifestyle. This is a constant in my life, and as sure as the tides.

For example, there are two ways to get to my office from my house. I live on Beverly Drive and my office is on El Camino. The fastest route is to go from Beverly down from my house into the business district, make a right on Wilshire, and go straight to my office door.

If I take one minute longer and I turn onto Canon and I go straight down Canon to my office door, it increases my visibility. It ups the chances of someone seeing me in my fabulous vintage car driving down the street, noticing me, noticing one of my FLAGG license plates. Then, a month later, they're getting ready to sell their home, thinking, "Oh, remember that guy? What's that guy's name, honey? He drives the gorgeous Rolls-Royce from the sixties or seventies?"

I keep some of my cars parked at the office, some at the house. I want everyone to know where I work and live. That's why I have the gardener change the flowers out front like a psychopath all the time. I want people to walk by and think, "Oh, that's the pretty house with all the flowers." The flowers don't need to be changed that often, but my goal is for them to constantly catch everyone's eye, like a department store window.

There's never a moment that my thoughts aren't on how I'm being perceived. (Yes. It can be exhausting to be me.)

A few nights ago, I came home at midnight after a drink . . . or three. I started rearranging the landscaping lighting to hit the blooms so they pop more vibrantly. People walk and drive by all the time. I want them to be drawn in by the flora, then see the house and license plates and put it all together that I live there. I want everything to telegraph the notion that if they worked with me, this could be their life too. Everything I do is to draw attention. Everything.

"Look at me, damn it" may well be the thesis statement for my life, largely because it works.

That's why when Claire and I pull up to my office this morning to pick up some documents after being at WOW studios, I make sure that everyone on the street sees me before I stroll inside. I hear a tourist say, "Hey, that's Josh Flagg!" and I swear to you, my day is made. I wave and say hello, and now the tourist and I are both smiling.

I'm a professional networker—okay, really, I'm more of a social climber, but I do it in a way that you'd never know I was social climbing. I know how to get into any door. Again, it all boils down to confidence. We're suspicious of the person who enters a place and projects anxiety, like they're about to be caught. Nervous, darting glances, fidgeting, an air of being obsequious, they're all dead giveaways that person doesn't belong. But no one stops the guy or gal who strides in like he or she owns the place. It's a matter of finesse.

The best advice is to always act like you've been there before, even if you haven't, regardless of circumstance.

For example, I'm not a member of a certain exclusive club—not because I can't be, but I just never joined. My family belongs to most of the important clubs, including Brentwood (humblebrag), but not this one. But I grew up coming here because both sets of grandparents were members. In fact, that's where my parents met during a forced set-up, masterminded by Edith. (That her plan worked speaks to Edith's own level of confidence.)

Anyway, when I walk in the door at the club, even though I don't technically belong, no one raises an eyebrow. The way I work a room and the way people come up to say hello from other tables—there's no question that I'm not a dues-paying member there. I just do it all with confidence, and that's the end of the story. No permission, no apologies.

"Cool, cool . . . confidence is great and all," you may say, "But how the hell do I find it inside myself when I don't feel it?"

You know the expression that action follows motivation? Personally, I think it's backward. Motivation comes only after you've undertaken the action. The same thing holds true for confidence. If you display confidence, you're going to start to feel it—it's the ultimate "fake it till you make it" scenario.

If you act confident, you'll become confident. Your motivation will follow your action.

Let me clue you in on what makes or breaks an effective dealmaker— the absolute belief that your product, service, or idea will improve the buyer's life or circumstances. (This is far easier if you follow my advice and sell something for which you're passionate.) Naturally, you want to make the deal because you'll get a check, which goes without saying. But if you look at a sale as the most expedient way to pay your bills and that's it, you're not set up for long-term success.

In my job, I'm confident approaching people because I'm certain that they'll be happier thanks to the windfall I get them when selling their home, or the improved quality of life they'll experience after buying one. (Remember, I don't sell garbage, and this is yet another reason why.)

I see myself as a conduit to improving my clients' lives. Think of it like this—if you knew how much better people would sleep at night having bought from you, wouldn't you feel incredible about yourself? Wouldn't you be fearless in approaching potential customers, excited even, secure in the knowledge that you can exponentially increase their contentment by solving a problem they didn't even know they had?

This mindset applies to any deal you might make, in any industry. For example, let's say you're trying to sell Cisco firewalls to an IT director. Before you ever go on a sales call, you'll have memorized all the product's impressive features and benefits and that's important. But your confidence (and commission) will increase as you understand and embrace the degree to which you're bettering the IT manager's life. You're now selling the inherent *advantages*, like the peace of mind that a network hack isn't going to drag that IT manager away from their daughter's wedding, that they're not going to pull their hair out trying to get support service, or that they won't be in trouble with the C-suite because of downtime during a migration. The advantages of the box far exceed the features and benefits that Cisco guarantees.

To make it more personal, let's circle back to Edith. Edith may have been the world's best dealmaker, even though her people skills could be . . . lacking. For example, she had a thick accent, so sometimes people asked her where she was from. Once time, a person then asked, "Where is Romania?" and Edith snapped, "Get a fucking globe!" But she didn't have to be charming to get the job done; her conviction was powerful enough on its own.

Edith thought my father was too old to be a bachelor. In her opinion, he wasn't going to progress in life without a wife, and his world would vastly improve after being wed. The only problem was, she didn't like the woman he was dating, so while my dad was on a ski trip, Edith moved her out. When he came home, she was gone. Edith had said to her, "You don't want to waste your time with my son. He is a playboy and never going to get married. I'll find you a more suitable guy."

Sounds nice, right? Wrong!

Edith had let herself into my dad's apartment and packed up all her things, moving her to a new apartment and prepaying her rent six months in advance before his return.

With the girlfriend situation handled, Edith then spent the week arranging dates with women she found more suitable. One of them was my mother. When my mom and Edith met at their country club, Edith practically pried open my mom's mouth to see her teeth, inspecting her up and down like a side of beef to make sure she was acceptable.

Turns out Edith was right; my parents were an ideal match, and they've been blissful together for decades. While it sounds like Edith would have been a total monster-in-law, she and my mother also had a wonderful relationship—likely because Edith picked her. Edith's conviction that my father needed the perfect wife proved true. That they would eventually make her a grandmother was a bonus in her book, and proof that she had plenty of self-interest too. And that's okay! Ultimately, she understood the advantages of my parents being together and worked doggedly to make it happen. She knew what was best for all involved and that belief gave her the confidence to meddle with impunity.

As for me, I get deals done because of my own utter faith that I'm doing what's best for my client by creating win-win scenarios in any room I enter, membership be damned.

FLAGG THIS

Assess the product, service, or idea you hope to sell. Look beyond the features and benefits—what are the advantages?

Use those advantages to build your confidence in your product and yourself.

For example, say you're selling a Japanese Global chef's knife.

The feature is the blade is thinner than its German counterparts, and the benefit is the blade size makes it ideal for more precise tasks, like slicing fish for sushi.

The advantage is a thin, hard blade means less sharpening, which not only saves time but also helps prevent the kind of accidents that stem from a dull knife; and no chef wants to tend to an injury in the middle of a dinner shift.

Suddenly, you're not pushing knives, you're protecting livelihoods. And doesn't that feel great?

///

TWENTY-ONE

Credibility Builds Confidence

B uild your confidence and distinguish yourself from the competition by establishing your bona fides. When I was starting out, I relied heavily on my family history, as I couldn't yet point to a successful track record or the wisdom that so often accompanies age. Credibility via nepotism is still credibility. (See: *Dynasties, Political Families; Kennedy and Bush.*)

Maybe I was just a teenager when I began my career, but I'm descended from people who helped shape the Los Angeles skyline. I was able to eke out credibility in the beginning because selling homes wasn't just business to me—it's a personal connection to all of Los Angeles. I'm a fourth generation Angeleno on my mother's side. My great-grandfather Benjamin Platt started Platt Music Corporation, and he built three buildings in downtown Los Angeles, one of which still has the Platt name on it. He used Walker & Eisen, the architects who are best known for designing the Beverly Wilshire Hotel.

Without the jumpstart my family afforded me, I would still be standing where I am; I'd just be a little older. I'm thankful for the path that my family paved before me. But if I couldn't deliver on that perceived credibility by knowing the luxury market—that is, understanding the pricing, being able to assess value, having inside knowledge of what a high-net-worth client wants, and so on—my career wouldn't have lasted long. My success is a byproduct of not only establishing credibility but then enhancing and cementing it through my actions.

FLAGG THIS

How have you established credibility, both personally and in your chosen field?

In what ways have you enhanced it?

If you're new to the business, reflect on what will help build your credibility without yet having a proven track record.

For example, did you spend every Saturday in the corner of an open house with a book, watching your mom crush it as a realtor in your small town? Did you hone your competitive spirit training for the Junior Olympics in track and field? Did you learn how to manage difficult people as a member of student government or the Greek system in college? Did you overcome your fear of rejection by spending a summer as one of those annoyingly earnest kids seeking petition signatures for an environmental cause?

And, if you're already established, how have you used your credibility to build on your successes?

TWENTY-TWO

Membership Has Its Privileges

I f you're confident and you have the right opening line—especially when presented in a familiar context—you'll often get what you want.

For instance, I was sitting at the Beverly Hills Hotel back when I was with a guy I had just started dating. In walked Mariah Carey. My date was obsessed with Mariah. While there's no way he was going to go up and talk to her, I scored major cool points because of the way I handled it.

Did I approach her and say, "Ms. Carey, my boyfriend loves you, can we have an autograph?"

That diva would have been like, "Get away, freak. I'm Mariah Carey."

The key to prompting someone to talk to you is that you need to give them what they want or what they can't have. Make them think there's something to be gained from talking to you.

So if I were to go up and say, "I don't want to be this person, but I've lived in this hotel for years," boom. That gets Mariah thinking, "Who is this guy? He can afford to live in this hotel. What's his story?" That statement makes her wheels turn and maybe she starts wondering if I'm the son of a big producer or someone else who can do something for her. It's how the game is played when you're a pro.

When I went up to Mariah's table, I was also kind of walking away at the same time, like I was almost too busy to be bothered. My attitude was, "I'm just saying hi as I'm passing, don't mind me." I wasn't stopping there and penning her in like a lunatic. Rather, I was just quickly offering some info as I swept by. The plan was to prompt *her* to invite *me* into the conversation to stay a little bit longer . . . and that's just what happened.

Turns out, Mariah had also lived in the hotel—that was the first thing she said. Having that commonality gave us a rapport.

Full disclosure: I didn't live in the hotel at the time. I had for a couple months previously, but she didn't have to know that. This wasn't about getting Mariah to like me—instead, it was about getting my date to. That was my true motivation.

By establishing the hotel resident connection, I'd come up with a shorthand way to let her know that we ran in similar circles, that there was no class disparity between us. I was able to speak to Mariah as an equal, not a fan, and that's intriguing for someone at her level. She wanted to know who I was, so when I said to my date, "Come over to the table, she'd be happy to say hello," that was the way that I did it.

Ultimately, my new beau met his idol because I was able to establish the fact that Mariah and I were in the same tribe.

In this case, we were tribe members because we're both divas—with that perfect nose, there's no way she's a Jew.

———— /// ————

TWENTY-THREE

Make an Entrance

Maybe Mariah liked me because she and I have something else in common; given the chance, we will always make an entrance. Making an entrance is part of my brand. While Bravo doesn't film 24-7, I live my life like there's always a camera on me.

For example, I go to temple once a year, and I walk in after the service starts, each time on purpose. That's because everyone's already sitting down and watching the rabbi. And when I walk in, the doors open and I come down the aisle like a maharaja. I do the whole "trying to be quiet" thing as I stroll to the front to sit with my family.

The lateness? Always intentional.

I play it off like I'm so embarrassed, but the reality is I've been standing around in back, waiting for the optimal moment to walk in. Of course, when I saunter in, I have the long tallit on and the kippah. I look very Jewish and proper, and I walk in and give respect to everyone when they try to talk to me as I head to take my seat. It's a lot of, "Shh, hi, great to see you, but we can't talk right now—it's Yom Kippur." (That's the day of atonement for the Jews and one of our holiest days.)

As I make my way to the front, I brush people off, all, "Please, focus on the rabbi, we'll talk later." Seats are assigned in the temple, and the closer you are to the bimah, the more money your family has given, so the Flaggs are in the first five rows. And I sit down at the front and then

I make noise, so people notice as I'm crossing the seats to sit down. Then I get into the service—I'm very focused because it actually is important to me.

Then I go up on stage afterward and the rabbi will say, "We're calling Josh Flagg for an aliyah," which means I do my prayer on stage. People think I have a good voice, so as I do my aliyah, people wave to me from the audience. The theatrics are all a marketing stunt, but I justify it because I funnel so much of my earnings back into Jewish charities. (More on that later.) I'm so shameless; I will take any opportunity to be noticed. #sorrynotsorry

As you establish yourself in sales, you'll begin to recognize patterns. You'll figure out which ponds stock the most fish metaphorically (unless you actually sell fish), and you'll continue to return to that spot. For me, my true honey hole is the Four Seasons Hotel in Maui.

On the surface, it doesn't make sense that the best place for me to drum up business would be almost twenty-five hundred miles away from where the homes I sell are located. But over the past ten years, I've made insane amounts of commission from the people I've met on vacation there.

I'm very social when I go anywhere—it's my nature. If I'm at the bar or just sitting around the pool, I talk to people. Everyone's chattier in a place like that because they're relaxed and unplugged. Even the biggest hard-asses loosen up with a Mai Tai in hand and the trade winds ruffling their hair.

My strategy here is no different than when I go to temple or to my office. I never take the quick way from my hotel room to pool, where no one sees me. I make the grand entrance where everyone can see me coming down the corridor. Just the other day, someone recognized me from an entrance I made at the Hotel du Cap.

I make myself a big presence when I walk in the room, the way I walk, the way I stand tall, the way I glide to the center of the room.

The key to making this strategy work is that I enter like I'm the most interesting person in the world, but once I start talking with someone, I treat them like *they're* the most fascinating. No one is ever bored when you're asking them about themselves, their experiences, their families, and so on.

As we talk, I establish our common ground. I love situations like this because there's so little I have to do to demonstrate how we're in the same tribe; just being there together establishes that fact.

I'm not advising you work the room like a used car salesman, passing out business cards like Halloween candy. Gross. Instead, be social and draw people to you. Make an impression. Be memorable. That way, when their friend in Beverly Hills says they're selling their home, the person I met will go, "You should call this guy I met in Maui." Mele kalikimaka!

FLAGG THIS

Where is your honey hole? Come up with three situations in which you could meet new people and tailor an opening line for each place.

Remember, there's potential business everywhere—maybe your next client is the gal sitting next to you in business class or the guy wearing the same parka as you at your kid's intramural hockey league. But you won't know if you don't talk to them, and you won't keep their interest if you can't relate to them.

TWENTY-FOUR

Let Me (E)state My Case

While a good attitude and confidence is important to have, none of that matters if you don't put these factors into play on the job. When I'm competing to list an estate, I might be pitted against up to ten other brokers, so it's crucial that my confidence is on point and that my message is ultraconsistent. These competitive situations usually happen when an elderly person passes away and a trust or the family is selling off the property. Instead of looking at the challenge as a chore, I relish the idea of going into battle with my peers. I can't be the best if I don't consistently beat the best.

The tone of my pitch will vary based on the personality of whomever I meet. The way I address an executor might be entirely different than how I'd speak with an owner's grandchild, but the content of my message doesn't change. Also, I'm perpetually confirming that with whomever I speak, we're of the same tribe and that I belong there. But before I even go into the appointment, I reflect on everything the potential seller needs to hear, and then it's my duty to hit every talking point once I'm in front of him or her.

When I have a listing appointment, I do my shtick. It's a performance. It's like a dance. And when I walk through a house, I float. I imagine I'm Oksana Baiul. I'm on ice. I'm floating. I'm dancing. I'm performing because it's a performance.

As I read the room, first, I take the temperature of the client. I figure out what kind of person they are by the questions I ask. Within a few minutes of gauging who they are, I adjust my approach accordingly. I become who they want and need me to be . . . kind of like a sociopath, but not in a bad way. Depending on the client, I might have to be a sports bro, a diva, a best friend, a drill sergeant—whatever it takes to get it done.

After I've figured out what the seller is like and the best way to connect with them, I go into those talking points. The first thing I stress is that I don't operate a huge team; it's just me. I emphasize that I don't have twenty-five thousand agents under me, so they're not going to shake my hand, sign the listing, and never see me again. I have too much pride in my reputation to stick them with some assistant or college lackey to run their open house. There will never be a time where I'd send a junior agent to sit in the foyer of a storied estate to greet people with a lazy, "Hi, if you, like, have any questions, let me know."

Unacceptable. I won't have my name associated with that lack of service.

I'm outraged when I bring a qualified buyer to an open house and I'm met by some gofer, fresh out of college. (If your last address was an ASU frat house, there's a 99 percent chance you're the wrong person to sell two acres in Trousdale. Fact. And yes, I realize I was in *high school* when I started, but I've also been thirty-five years old my entire life.) My point is, what are these big brokers doing when they're too busy to show a $20 million estate themselves? They're not out there making commensurate sales because I'd know about them.

Anyway, I tell the seller that they're going to get *me* selling their property. I state this reality many different times and ways. (Did you notice?) Studies show the average person must hear something at least seven times before committing that piece of info to fact. We remember because of repetition and the more someone hears a specific detail or feature, the more likely they are to believe it. Advertisers use this trick extensively. You know how sometimes you'll watch a streaming show and you'll see the same commercial three times in a row? That's not a mistake.

FLAGG THIS

Say it once, say it twice, but saying it seven times is nice.

I make sure the seller understands they're going to get my phone number so they can call me any time. There's no reason I'd ever be un-reachable for more than a few minutes—I live and die by my phone. I literally dive on my phone when it rings because it could be money calling.

I don't have an ego about not selling my listings myself. I want to be in the mix. I get those listings because I'm dying to be the one who presents them to a buyer, because no one will have done their homework like me. If a seller signs with me, they get me. End of story.

I like to remind potential sellers, "You're paying me a lot of money for my service, so you're damn well going to get me. You deserve my full attention." That's so important to stress . . . and wouldn't be believable if not delivered with confidence.

Why do I do this?

It's not because clients are paying me too much—they aren't. I know my worth. Instead, I'm stressing the value of my services. If they pay less, they get less. Saying the quiet part out loud actually builds trust because I'm acknowledging to the seller than I know—and will handle—my shit.

Specifically telling sellers I'm expensive is a baller move that works. Look at it this way—do you want to get rhinoplasty from a plastic sur-geon who boasts about having the lowest prices, or will you be more confident with the doctor who is unapologetic about their fees? There are places you just do not want to cut corners, and real estate is one of them.

I land the estate listings almost every time because I have such a track record with them. Ironically, in the past, I was less likely to get the lower-priced listings. It wasn't until I started soliciting feedback that I was able to course correct.

How do I course correct?

I politely ask why the seller didn't go with me. It's such a small, low-stakes step, but so telling. A lot of times, people really wanted to work with me, but I didn't give them the reassurance that they needed because I didn't verbalize it.

What I learned was I needed to start explaining to those homeowners that I sell more than just estates and if I take on their listing, they'll get an equal amount of attention. Their house is just as important as the sprawling estate on the hill. The lower-priced homes are my bread and butter because I sell them every day, so I assure sellers that they are a priority too. In my head, I always knew that, but I didn't always verbalize it, and not taking this extra step cost me listings. I should have known that if *I* didn't reassure the seller, who would? Now this guarantee is baked into my pitch.

Through soliciting feedback on failed listings, I learned that I needed to adjust my enthusiasm level. Even the pros benefit from upping their attitudes. I made the error of being too low key when touring potential listings because I wanted to seem cool.

Huge mistake on my part.

If the seller doesn't see my enthusiasm, how are they supposed to feel it? A blasé attitude does no one any favors. Who wants to work with a jaded broker? No one!

Now, in addition to knowing my stuff, I make sure that I'm projecting my excitement. Sellers need to feel it. I used to walk in and expect to get a listing—this was a massive failing. Today, I show buyers how much I love their homes by my facial expressions. What sucks is I can never get Botox because I'm afraid I won't project the proper amount of excitement if my forehead doesn't move.

Still, it's a sacrifice I'm willing to make—that's how much I want everyone's listings.

Now, an ideal listing situation for me is meeting a client with a sense of humor. Somebody in their sixties and above, Jewish, lives in Beverly Hills. If they're in their seventies? Even better! I love working with people who remember things from Beverly Hills from any time up to the 1990s, which is so ironic because I'm nostalgic for a time period I never experienced.

I love listings with clients who are older because once you get to a certain age, you cut through all the bullshit and posturing. People stop being so competitive once they reach a certain point in life. Yeah, I'll be whomever the client needs me to be, but I'm happiest around the ones who allow me to be me.

While I enjoy all parts of the process, given a choice, I'd prefer to represent a buyer over a seller. For a listing, you're obligated to wait for the magical person to show up, and a lot of that has to do with the pricing on the home. But I'd rather work with a buyer because this allows me more creativity. I excel at identifying properties for the right person. So I like to show off my skills to these people, and I'm always pretty spot-on. And I prefer the pacing of working with buyers—the process is generally quicker. I will say I like working with a buyer more because I'm good at gauging people's wants and needs. If someone tells me they want to be in X location for Y price with Z bedrooms, I can point out the house in one minute. Very few brokers succeed because they don't listen to what the buyer wants. I listen and I deliver, and that's because I know my shit better than anyone. I will inherit clients from other brokers so often, and they will say to me, "I like working with you because you nailed it in one second."

But regardless of whether I'm working with a buyer or a seller, my attitude always matters.

//

Age, Attitude, and Arrogance

I don't care what stage of your career you're in, you're going to make mistakes. They're unavoidable. The goal is that you use the experience to strengthen yourself as a dealmaker. At the very least, the hope is you don't keep doing the same thing wrong over and over, because that's just sloppy.

Don't be sloppy.

I started my career with an enormous, college-sized chip on my shoulder. Couple the arrogance with a lack of maturity, shake it with ice, and I served up a toxic cocktail of ego and insecurity sure to sicken the whole crowd. (A Flaggtini, if you will.)

If you want to up your attitude, start to self-reflect. Look back on where you've been professionally and make an honest assessment. You won't be able to strengthen your weak spots until you determine what they are.

I'm well aware of the areas in which I was lacking . . . because I can stream the early seasons of *Million Dollar Listing Los Angeles* and relive them all.

Yay.

Once I stop wincing at my acid-washed denim lewks, I can cringe over the moments when my ego indeed landed. I was so arrogant that I couldn't help but try to rub in every success, at all the wrong moments. Mind you, this is a competitive business, and we're all proud of our wins, but I would take it to the nth degree. For a while, I suspect everyone thought my name was Josh F'ing Flagg.

The satisfaction in my accomplishments should have been enough; they were not. In my early days, I needed everyone to celebrate me, even when my success had come at their loss. I've long since learned it's not cool to force my achievements down the throats of those just trying to get through their day, like an unsuspecting foie gras goose.

My issue was, I took what was a bit of beginner's luck and eventually turned it into a true career, based on skill and knowledge. But along the way, I burned a lot of bridges by conflating this early luck with my own prowess. Oops.

I went into my career with the attitude that failure was not an option . . . except it totally was. If I didn't make it as a realtor, I wasn't going to be homeless or hungry or without Hermès. My family was an impenetrable safety net, but I neither recognized, acknowledged, nor appreciated this fact. You know the expression, "What would you do if you knew you couldn't fail?" That sums up my life, except I had no clue as I'd never experienced anything else. I still worked like my safety and security depended on it, and I expected the kudos for when it worked out exactly like I'd planned. Let me say this—it's a hell of a lot easier to get to home plate when you're starting on third base.

FLAGG THIS

What about you? What happens if your plans don't work out? Will it all be over? Will you be homeless? Will you be unable to dust yourself off and try again?

While my prowess would eventually come with experience, I didn't recognize this fact when I was still basking in my early victories. So I was out there shooting off my mouth, trying to tell the seasoned brokers how they were all doing it wrong, and I was the only one who had it right.

This made me exactly as unpopular as you might imagine.

Here's the thing—more than one person can excel at a job, and they can each do it in their own way. Styles differ. There's no single path to success, yet my hubris got in the way of my understanding and accepting this fact. That's why when I would screw up in the beginning, like taking too many high-end listings and not pricing them right, my competition reveled when they were able to snatch those listings back from me.

It was humbling.

While it doesn't feel like it, I realize I'm fortunate for having had so many of my early missteps caught on camera. Sure, they made for entertaining reality television, but those instances were just that—reality. I made a lot of enemies in the beginning. To this day, there are luxury brokers in L.A. who will go out of their way to avoid having to work with me, and that's to my detriment, as well as my clients and theirs. I thought being young and successful gave me a license to misbehave.

Spoiler alert: it did not, and I'm still repairing that damage.

For example, once a week, everyone goes on what's called a Brokers Caravan. We all travel from open house to open house during a set time, seeing what's new on the market. During these events, everyone parks on the street. But I was obnoxious in the beginning. I'd park in the middle of the driveway so everyone would have to walk around my car and they couldn't help but see my vanity plate that read FLAGG1 on that luxury vehicle. I was trying to rub my success in their faces. I thought it was hilarious, but it just made other brokers resent me.

While I still pull these stunts on camera, the difference is, now when I do it, it's for entertainment and not to anyone else's detriment. (Also, because I'm not great at parking, it's funny, and I want the camera to catch my plates.)

Still, I was too shortsighted to see that my arrogance cost me money because people were less willing to meet me in the middle for deals.

Occasionally, I'll reflect on the ways that college might have helped me develop softer skills. If I'd ever gotten my ass kicked as a fraternity pledge, I might not have been so cocky from the jump. And maybe four years of higher learning would have given me more maturity when I started in the business.

I don't have regrets, but I can see a universe where taking a little time before I started in real estate could have been helpful. I mean, I've never had any other job. I never folded jeans at the Gap, never took anyone's drink order. I was never a summer lifeguard, never flipped a burger. Doing so may have given me some humility, and that lack hurt me when I was starting out.

I used to walk into brokers' open houses like I owned the place, not being humble at all. (There's a difference between making a fabulous entrance and being a douche—learn to recognize the line.) Or I'd call other agents when they lost a deal, like a listing expired, and I'd jump on their clients, trying to get the listing right away. Douchebag, party of one.

I learned the hard way that buyers come and they go, but brokers are forever. So you never want to have a bad relationship with them. I don't recommend it, but you can screw over a client without major recourse. You'll never hear from them again, but it's not the worst thing that could happen. But if you screw over a broker, especially one who's big in the business and has substance and longevity?

You're never going to make a deal with them again.

Before I got on the show, I felt like I was a celebrity, so it didn't help my attitude once I became one. When I landed the show, my attitude was, "Hello, I've been waiting for this." In my head—and in my behavior—nothing changed. My first couple seasons are a bit cringeworthy, especially those awful Dior sunglasses I was sporting. Oy.

Thank God I had Edith there to show that I had a softer side.

Bill Murray once said, "When you become famous, you've got like a year or two where you act like a real asshole. You can't help yourself. It happens to everybody. You've got like two years to pull it together—or it's permanent."

In my experience, people tend to have short-term memories. I burned a lot of bridges and I regret them. But I guess once you reach a certain level of success, people either forget about it because they want to be your friend, or they want to be in business with you. They need your business, and they still think you're a piece of shit, but they put a smile on their faces because they know they need you.

My hope with the relationships I've repaired is that it's not because of the latter.

English novelist Catherine Aird once said, "If you can't be a good example, then you'll just have to be a horrible warning."

So I guess I'd advise that the best way to up your attitude is to err on the side of being a good example.

Still, not every cocky move I made was the wrong one. When I was in the early days of my career, I spent a lot of time soliciting press coverage because the best advertising is free advertising. Because I was "helpful," I'd draft the articles for the reporters, skewing each answer for maximum benefit

I was younger than almost every broker, so I pitched that as a feature, not a flaw. I didn't want buyers to perceive my age as a weakness, so I would proactively counter these objections in these articles. For example, I'd write the questions I was supposedly answering as, "Does being so young hurt you?" Then I'd respond with an emphatic, "Hell, no! Being young is the best thing that could happen and it's my reason for success. I have youthful energy, and I bring new ideas to a staid industry. If you think about it, people pay far more attention to youthful achievements versus old. If a fifty-year-old sells a $20 million property? That's nice, good for them. But if a nineteen-year-old does it? That's why you're writing about me!"

Of course, when I'm ninety and still selling multimillion dollar properties, you can be damn sure I'll still be publicizing them. The headlines will read: "World's Oldest Working Realtor Sells L.A.'s Most Expensive

Home." But hopefully I'll still have plenty of friends in the business who want to help me celebrate it.

FLAGG THIS

How would you spin your perceived flaws or weaknesses to a reporter? How would you rewrite that narrative?

—— /// ——

TWENTY-SIX

My Go-To Attitude Adjustment

Things go wrong sometimes, as I've said. Houses fall out of escrow. Clients can betray me. I might make a social media faux pas. Bad days happen to us all. I've found the best way for me to adjust my attitude is to go back to my roots. If I need a boost, I'll return to what always brought me success in the beginning of my career—I'll knock on doors.

Do I make door knocking sound easy? Well, it is if you have the right mindset. I refer you again to the Mormon kids out serving missions, running around in their black flood pants and white shirtsleeves. They will knock on your door day or night, and they're thrilled for the opportunity because they believe it's God's will. Sure, having a sales quota is pressure, but imagine how hard you'd work if you thought *the Lord* was your boss.

Given the confidence it takes to knock, you'll be surprised at who will talk to you if you have the right things to say.

"Well, Josh," you might reply, "things were a lot different than when you were out knocking on doors." Oh, you mean on *Sunday*, because I still do it. If things start to feel slow or just too heavy, I always default to going to someone's door. It's my secret weapon.

Last week, I was on Green Acres Drive, next to the Harold Lloyd estate. I saw a promising house, and I said to the friend who was with me, "We should ring the bell and see what happens. Let's see if we can get a listing out of it."

I started the conversation with the goal to immediately put the home-owner at ease. I wanted to make her comfortable. I said, "Hi, this is Josh Flagg."

Then I paused for a second to see if she recognized me from the show.

While it sounds like a conceited move, I'm really gauging how I approach the conversation. I'm always golden if they know my name, but you don't have to be on television to make that happen. If you're diligent about hitting an area with marketing material, there's a good chance potential clients will recognize your name. Maybe your flyer is taped to their fridge right now because they'd meant to request an estimate on whatever you're selling. Who knows, right?

In this case, the pause passed without recognition, but no problem. I said, "I'm your neighbor, I live on the 600 block of Beverly Drive." So now what was she thinking? Probably, "Oh, 600 block of Beverly Drive. Okay, I can be nice to this person; he's rich because he lives on the 600 block of Beverly."

Having money is not the point of this example. What's important is that I established my credibility by mentioning why I belonged there.

This is crucial.

For example, let's say you're an ex-military MP and now you're working in an industry that sells personal protection products to law enforcement. You lead off with that connection. You immediately establish yourself as someone who speaks their language. Humans are tribal beings, by nature. We feel most secure when we're able to identify someone else on our team, because outsiders are threatening.

Figure out what your connection is to your potential client and open with that. LinkedIn profiles are a smart place to research this, as are mutual Facebook contacts. Everyone wants to connect with a fellow Boilermaker or Trojan or Horned Frog or whatever your weird-ass college mascot was. You probably have friends in common, and if they're rude to you, they're going to feel pretty damned stupid when you bump into them at Sully's next tailgate.

Establish that common ground in the first breath so they can let down their guard. (Unless you are a serial killer. *This advice is not for you, Dahmer.*)

Anyway, I did just that. The resident immediately knew I was "one of us." She replied, "Hi, Josh, what can I do for you?" I said, "So I'm your neighbor," again, always reinforcing that connection, "and I just wanted to mention to you that I have a friend in the car and we're out looking for houses. Now, please, if it's not something you're interested in, please, please, I don't want to take any more of your time, don't let me interrupt your Sunday."

At this point, I hadn't mentioned I was a real estate agent. But I could tell she knew I was a real estate agent, which meant it was okay because she *was* familiar with who I was. Yes!

I explained how my friend was looking for a house on at least an acre, like hers, and we just started chatting from there. None of this was face-to-face, all of it over the intercom. We spoke for half an hour, while my friend listened in, fascinated.

I found out the homeowner had seen the show and she loved Edith, plus we had mutual friends, *exactly as I predicted*. Long story short, because I was immediately able to identify myself as a member of her tribe, she was willing to listen to what I had to say. We set up a dinner and I'll meet her next week.

Because I've only spoken with her via intercom, I'll figure out who she is at the restaurant in the usual way.

No, not Google-stalking.

It's more fun for me to find out the old-fashioned way, like I'd have to do before internet searches. I like to walk in and make eye contact with other people in the room. You see if they do that little take when they go, "Oh, you're the person, right, nice to meet you." It's a guessing game, plus it's a fun way to get other new people to talk to me, too. There's an old adage that goes, "It's easier to ask for forgiveness than to beg for permission," and ultimately, it's a smart way to end up talking to people I wasn't intended to meet.

I plan on doing this exact thing at tonight's dinner, where I finally come face to face with Anastasia, my Betsy Bloomingdale to the nth degree. A white whale. My Moby Dick. Just thinking about our meeting fills me with dual shots of anticipation and anxiety, a bittersweet combination of emotions. So, call me Ishmael . . . and we'll get to that part later.

Anyway, when I do meet my potential new client from the door-knocking exercise, I'm confident that she will be happier because my selling her home will improve her life.

And who doesn't want to be happier?

PART FOUR

––– /// –––

Be the Billionaire

To negotiate truly high-end deals, having confidence is not enough; you must put yourself into a billionaire's shoes.

I know it may sound corny, but if you come at every deal like you're a billionaire, you won't be too intimidated to fight for what you need. A real billionaire would never get hung up on the small stuff it's taken to get them there, such as advertising and marketing costs, or the expense of paying for a team; so you shouldn't, either. The saying you must spend money to make money holds true.

Remember this—a billionaire who's selling their $10 million vacation home doesn't care whether they

make the deal or not. So the only way to get that contract signed and squeeze every penny out of it is to
react in kind and pretend that you, another billionaire,
have nothing to lose, either.

———— /// ————

TWENTY-SEVEN

My Favorite Billionaire

Edith taught me to live like a billionaire, taking me to more than seventy countries during her lifetime. Also, I should mention that while I worshipped her, Edith wasn't one of those soft, passive nanas who baked muffins for her grandkids. In fact, when I was just a toddler, she stopped me from calling her "grandma," telling me, "My name is Edith." That was a fond memory.

Edith and I traveled all over the world together. Experiencing how other cultures live shaped the way I conduct my life. While I'm all about hard work, the job has its time and place. When it comes to vacation, I embrace how Europeans do it, taking off anywhere from four to six weeks. Per the *New York Times*, Americans average about 1,804 hours of work per year, which is almost fifty percent more than Germans, French, and Italians. Could I make more money if I put in more hours? Of course. But being miserable isn't worth it. If you want to excel, find a sweet spot between work and play . . . exactly like billionaires do.

Edith was also the inspiration for closing my first six-figure deal when I was twelve, believe it or not.

I was browsing eBay for French silk pajamas, and I ran across what I felt could be a profitable investment. Business acumen is a valued trait in my family, and I hoped to prove that even though I was a kid, I was savvy. I wanted my parents to see I'd been paying attention and that I'd learned how to spot opportunities to make money too. From an early age, I wanted to be the billionaire.

My plan was to surprise them by winning the auction, so I didn't mention it beforehand. I didn't want to disappoint them if I couldn't make it happen. Because the auction item could end up being pricey, I was required to provide proof of funds to bid, beyond the emergency credit card my parents had given me. I liked that eBay wanted to filter out the riffraff, to keep away those who weren't serious buyers. So I went to my dad's checkbook and wrote down all his banking information, then provided it to eBay.

Like that, I was off to the races!

I babysat that auction for days, conscious of every dollar increase in bidding. We didn't have the internet on phones yet, so I ran to the computers in my school's library between each class to check on the auction's status. My hands would sweat every time I increased my bid, adrenaline coursing through me. I had to win—it was my birthright. I had a sleepless night before the auction ended, my tired, bloodshot eyes never leaving the computer screen. My hand cramped as I kept my fingers poised on my mouse, poised to click into action.

My diligence paid off and I won the auction! I was the proud new owner of . . . a 1937 Mercedes-Benz Roadster.

My God, this was a beautiful machine, sleek and shiny, low slung, and curvy as a woman, with custom coachwork fitted by Mayfair Carriage Co. The car had fender skirts and polished louvers, an elegance long since missing in modern automotive manufacturing.

I could just imagine myself in this car, top down, zipping through the streets of Monte Carlo, white walls and chrome wheels spinning. Supercharged with an eight-cylinder engine and vacuum-assisted hydraulic brakes, this beauty was built for sustained cruising, making for a powerful, yet luxurious ride. The Roadster was the most expensive and exclusive automobile of its time, and what made it extra special were its armored sides and bulletproof glass. But the protective elements didn't seem like overkill—after all, the car had belonged to Adolf Hitler.

That's right—the item I tried so hard to win was Hitler's Mercedes.

I felt that not only was this a sound investment, but I loved the idea of driving my grandmother around in it. What better way to rub the Nazis' loss in their faces by taking a tiny Jewish Dutch Resistance fighter to lunch at the Polo Lounge in it?

I was so proud of myself when I was finally able to share with my family what I'd done. I marched down the stairs and announced, "We just bought Hitler's Mercedes!"

My parents? They were less "proud" and more "shocked" with a side of "horrified."

Not only did they *not* see the vehicle as a worthwhile investment, but they did not care to bring any Nazi memorabilia into our home. They weren't big fans of my forking over $250K either.

My mother is an attorney, and she spent a month arguing precedence with eBay and the car company. Through surprisingly complex legal wrangling, she proved that a child was not qualified to purchase a 1937 car that had previously transported members of the Third Reich, and we weren't forced to take delivery. She argued a twelve-year-old could not afford the leader of the Third Reich's car.

Even Edith was disappointed in me, but not for the reasons you'd imagine. She was upset because I'd conflated Adolf Hitler and Heinrich Himmler (the actual owner), and I hadn't paid enough attention to the Holocaust education she'd been giving me my whole life. That summer, we toured concentration camps to cement my knowledge, and I came back with a burning desire to do more for my people.

Fortunately, enough time has passed that my parents laugh about the incident now. When they do, they refer to it as Hitler's Mercedes, even though it's not technically correct.

The great irony here is, I was right; the car was a sound investment. Back in 2016, a similar 1937 Mercedes Roadster went for $9.9 million at auction.

Presumably, it did not sell to a twelve-year-old.

‡‡‡

It Takes a Village

While I'm technically a one-man operation, I can't do everything myself. Being able to scale in a sales career requires proper support. Ask yourself, "If I'm stuck in the office filling out forms, who's going to be out there selling?" By not taking a portion of your earnings and bringing in help, you're wasting your own best resources.

Listen, I understand that the salesperson wants to maintain control on every aspect of their business, but at a certain point, it's necessary to bring in people you trust to help.

Every billionaire got to where he or she is now by investing in personnel. So many companies claim to have gotten their starts in a garage—I'm talking Apple, Microsoft, Google, HP, and Amazon. The notion of being a garage start-up is part of the mystique of each of these lauded organizations. Obviously, these industry titans are not run out of garages now, and one of the reasons for that is you can only fit so many people in a one-car bay.

You want growth? You want to be a billionaire like Jeff Bezos or Steve Wozniak? It takes a village.

My village grows as my business expands. Claire is my personal assistant, and she's with me most of the time. Hilary is a former assistant, and now she's the director of operations—she runs more of the real estate aspect. (I'm not the only one trying to be the billionaire here.) I'm bringing in another person to assist Claire, so I'll have an assistant to my assistant, and she'll do more house-management duties. I love the idea of that—it's so Miranda Priestly. I should start throwing my coat at her.

Wait. Claire says she is not on board with my throwing coats at anyone. Also, when was the last time anyone wore a coat in L.A.?

Anyway, when I land a listing, the whole team springs into action. Hilary will introduce herself and send paperwork and set up photography for the marketing material. In the interim, I may arrange a Brokers' Price Opinion, if we're not yet sure on price. Between the rest of the team, they'll work out the minutia, like coordinating with the videographer and photographer and stager. There's no reason for me to be involved with those details, as I trust them to vet everyone; they know my standards.

Once the marketing photos are back, I do take over. I will personally go through all the shots, and I'll write the descriptions—this step is directly related to selling, so I won't outsource these tasks. Nothing is printed or published until I've made and proofed every selection, because I'm that diligent about what's attached to my name.

A lot of real estate marketing brochures will include fifty to sixty photos. I don't like the kitchen sink approach; I won't throw in everything. I want my marketing material to draw buyers in (see: *Gretel, Hansel and*), not tell them everything they need to know without ever setting foot in the house. And I arrange my photos in a way that tells a story. I've said it again and again—stories make sales. When you invest in yourself, and build out your infrastructure, you'll be on your way too.

Because I happen to be home, I decide to join Hilary and Claire as they interview someone to fill the dual roles of Claire's assistant/my house manager.

The agency we use thoroughly screens applicants first, a tremendous time-saver. They've sent through several ideal candidates, so the process is more about picking the absolute best fit. I was recently burned by a former assistant who felt that denigrating me on camera was a solid career move—it was not—so we're applying extra scrutiny this time around.

Working for me entails more than just possessing certain competencies; it's about being adaptable and having a positive attitude. That person isn't obligated to laugh at my jokes (again, see: *Claire, Hilary and*), but he or she must patiently manage chaos and ever-changing duties. I need someone who's nimble, quick, ready to solve problems. Plus, this person should have the confidence to challenge me and keep me on track if he or she notices that my ADHD has kicked in and I'm target-focusing on one thing for too long. (Whining about me to a documentary crew? Not one of the job's duties.) For all these things, they're paid well above the market standard.

If you want the best people? You must compensate them accordingly.

We've already found a woman who I believe is the right fit. Her background is solid, but more important, she seems to *get* us and already feels like one of the team. But there's still someone the agency wants us to meet. I voted we just cancel the interview and make the offer to the person we all loved, but Hilary and Claire overruled me, as they liked this applicant's résumé.

The woman arrives early (nice) and greets us with confidence (also nice). She reminds me of a younger version of Heather Dubrow from *The Real Housewives of Orange County*, sleek and polished and peppy, seemingly well-acquainted with the luxury marketplace and the finer things in life. I feel like I wouldn't need to explain the differences in thread counts to her. (No, we can't just buy sheets off Amazon.com, you monster.) She's dressed in skintight workout wear, which would be inappropriate anywhere but the 90210. Here, it's more like a uniform.

We settle in the living room to talk. Cute Applicant has served as a personal assistant as well as a live-in babysitter in the homes of some producers and directors. Looks like she's handled many of the duties we'd need, so maybe it's good Hilary and Claire insisted we give her a chance. I've certainly been wrong before.

We ask Cute Applicant to summarize her experience. I want to hear her describe her favorite parts of her other jobs, because in a real employment situation, I know she'd gravitate toward those tasks. When I interviewed Claire, she practically glowed describing the ways she helped organize her last employer and the systems she streamlined, binders and tabs and Gantt charts, oh, my! This was exactly what I'd hoped to hear and consistently what she's delivered.

Cute Applicant tells us all about what a great relationship she's had with her employers, literally every member, like a part of the family! When we ask about her organizational experience, she details the ways she's whipped the husbands' home offices into shape. When we query about her party-planning skills, she tells us all about the spectacular fiftieth birthday bash she orchestrated for one of her employers' father, her handprint on every one of the smallest details, including a tasting flight of all his favorite Scotches. As for coordinating my wardrobe, no problem! She routinely shopped with the husbands, guiding them to the best purchases and then managing their closets.

Her entire pitch focuses on how she makes life so much easier for the families she works for, just a real Girl Friday, filling in for any duty the lady of the house can't manage. When she says her aim is to be like a second wife, I choke back a laugh and Claire frowns at me.

We speak for about ten minutes and Cute Applicant has no questions, so she excuses herself and leaves.

"Just me, or was that weird?" Hilary asks.

"So weird. She dismissed us," Claire adds, shaking her head. "I allotted an hour for this interview. She wasn't even here fifteen minutes! I wonder what happened?"

What happened was, Cute Applicant quickly assessed she had zero chance to become the next Mrs. Joshua D. Flagg.

I explain, "Ladies, have we learned nothing from Ben Affleck and Gavin Rossdale?"

"What?" Hilary asks.

"Never hire the hot nanny."

Every billionaire who can say "community property state" would agree.

TWENTY-NINE

The Billionaire's Network

Any billionaire worth his or her salt understands how to seamlessly mesh their business and social lives. Here's a perfect example: A while back, I had a dinner with Jeff Lewis, Heather McDonald, and Melissa Rivers. We were at Craig's, which is a popular restaurant in L.A. After we finished, I wasn't ready to go home. Because I'm so ADHD, I always want to stay out. I didn't want to just go home and go to bed.

So I walked inside and did a loop, like always. I examined the territory. I read the room. I saw who was there, saw where I could pick up business. Sometimes it works, and sometimes I just sit with friends.

On this night, I spotted my buddies Roxy and Christie sitting there, so I sat down with them. Eventually, the maître d' of the Gucci restaurant came up to me to say hello. She invited me to her table, as she had some friends in town who were looking for a house.

One of her pals was a woman from Miami. She told me, "This realtor showed me around; we've been looking at $10 million houses," and frankly, that sounded too good to be true. Who just goes to dinner and comes home with a multimillion-dollar deal?

After I found out all about the potential client—what she loves, hates, can't live without, and so on—we scheduled an appointment to look at homes in the Palisades and Montecito. But we didn't go see them because she never confirmed. I could have chalked the whole thing up as having been too good to be true, but I couldn't let an opportunity pass without another try.

I reached out to her again and she was so glad to hear from me! It turns out she'd emailed me three days earlier, but her note had gone to my spam file. She said she figured I was too busy for her. She admitted she didn't want to be too aggressive because she said she didn't want to embarrass herself on television.

She said, "So I have this broker. I don't like him. He took us to see this house in the Palisades, but he's too busy on the golf course to bother to return my call."

Now, I would be furious if I showed a buyer a house and they didn't use me to make an offer. But because I keep my client list manageable, this doesn't happen. So I told her, "That's horrible! He's on the golf course and doesn't have time for you. Unacceptable."

I went out the next morning, sealed the deal, and now we're in escrow on this house. So essentially, a dinner that cost me $180 turned into a $100,000 commission, minus a healthy finder's fee for my friend at Gucci.

Here's the thing—I advertise a lot. People call me because I send mailers. And I'm ubiquitous in Beverly Hills, so people know me. Plus, I get referrals from people I've worked with. Business can come from so many different directions and being on TV only helps with recognition.

FLAGG THIS

How does your friend network enhance your dealmaking?

If I didn't live the billionaire-style life, however, and maintain the friendships I have, I'd still miss opportunities. If I didn't embody my brand, I wouldn't know the maître d' from Gucci. I wouldn't have been invited to that table. If I'd just been lazy and ordered from Postmates, saving $150 off the cost of my dinner, I'd have missed out on $100,000.

The lesson here is that the more social you are, the more people you'll have in your social circle. When you have a group of people thinking of you, rooting for you, actively promoting you, the sky's the limit.

For me, there's no line between my professional and social lives; they are inexorably mixed. My goal as a broker is to do such a good job that people want to keep me in their lives, and this happens all the time. In fact, I recently went on vacation with clients. (They were sober. Yeah, I didn't sign up for that part of the trip, but I made do.)

My social connections recently led me to showing Kim Kardashian's house. She was lovely and sweet, but I swear to you, her butt is so big, it has its own gravitational pull.

Thus far, she has not opted to become my friend. Her loss.

At least, that's what I tell myself.

—— /// ——

THIRTY

Spend Money
to Make Money

One of my greatest assets as a dealmaker is the exposure from being on Bravo. The show has opened so many opportunities by creating a situation where buyers can find me, instead of vice versa. Because *MDLLA* gives me tremendous reach, I use it to my full advantage.

For example, I'm involved with a garden charity. Am I the only man involved in this charity because I grow my own flowers and tomatoes?

Ugh, no. I don't want to get my hands dirty; I just had a manicure. So why am I part of it?

Well, do you know what garden charities attract? That's right, fabulously wealthy women of a certain age, clad in Chanel suits and dripping in jewelry and discernment . . . basically my favorite type of people ever.

To help promote our work, I invited a group of twelve older ladies associated with the charity out to lunch with me. The kicker was, we'd put that scene on the show. The women loved it and we had a blast filming together.

The scene was meant to be a comedic element, "Oh, look at Josh surrounded by all these Golden Girls telling him what to do!" Honestly, the day was a riot, especially because the women were tremendous sports. While everyone likes to see me argue with Altman or swan around a mansion, this lunch was a fun diversion from the norm for all involved.

But I do nothing without a reason; I'm too calculating for that. What you didn't see on television afterward was the goodwill I built up. Thanks to the event, I ended up selling to the women in the group over the years, including a $10 million listing, all for the cost of a $1,000 lunch.

Here's the thing—you don't need to be a billionaire to maximize chances to sell more. (Doesn't hurt, but it's not necessary.) The fact is, wherever you are in your sales career, if you just supplement the tools you already possess—your confidence, creativity, and in my case, cunning—with a couple bucks and a posse who has your back, the sky's the limit.

FLAGG THIS

Imagine yourself employed in the following situations:

- Working part time in a local women's clothing boutique
- Calling on cardiologists as a pharmaceutical rep
- Selling educational software to school districts

What advantages do you personally possess that would assist you in each of these diverse sales jobs?

Think about it . . . maybe you have an Instagram presence. Perhaps your wife is a nurse.

Possibly you have children in school.

Take a step back and look at the connections you possess right now.

How would you use the tools you have at hand (meaning a small budget and a dedicated friend group) to help create the impetus to move these products?

Here's an even better example of where I spent a few dollars and created a windfall.

A while back, I met a woman named Amber who came to see a house I had for lease. She was looking for a place for her daughter. I say this all the time, I'm willing to work on leases specifically because they can lead to so many opportunities. While her daughter chose another property, I made enough of an impression that Amber remembered me.

One day, I was at the Bailey's Beverly Hills Hotel coffee shop having breakfast. When my schedule allows it, I try to eat outside of my house because of the social aspect. I ran into Amber there and I invited her to join me.

After I paid our tab, Amber told me, "My husband and I are considering selling our house in the future," so she invited me to see her place in Bel Air.

This breakfast led me to not only sell her Bel Air place for $16 million but also to help her purchase another home.

Amber and her husband loved a listing that had just hit the market. The property was priced right and wouldn't last the weekend. She asked, "How do we get it?" and I said, "Well, it's quite simple. We give them an offer, all cash, close in three days, no inspections. Obviously, the seller will jump on that. It's a calculated risk, buying a place with no inspection, but it's the key to getting the deal done quickly."

Because they're billionaires and they wanted the home, they agreed to the terms and the deal was done.

It was baller.

A week went by, and Amber called me, saying, "We need to talk to you." Oh, no! I started second-guessing myself. I thought I was clear about the risks of buying without an inspection, but what if they changed their minds? I hated the idea of them being angry or disappointed.

I took the couple out for sushi and conversation, bracing myself for the Mack truck that was going to hit me next.

Very gently, Amber broke the news to me. "We don't want you to be upset with us, but we want you to sell that new house." They'd changed their mind, not about *buying* the house but about *living* in the home they'd bought.

The couple were worried they'd offend me, like they were returning a present I'd bought them.

Offend me? A second commission? Trust me, not offended.

I said, "Okay, let's try to get you out of there."

I put that house back on the market and was able to sell it for a couple hundred thousand dollars higher, so they walked away with a profit. That's not easy to do. I sold them another property a week later on Perugia. They kept it for a brief time and then had me sell it, because they decided they didn't want it, either. (If you're wondering what kind of people like putting all their shit in boxes to move, don't worry—they didn't end up living in either of the homes.)

When all was said and done and we finally settled the couple in the place they wanted, I ended up doing about $48 million in transactions with them, earning close to $1.3 million in commission over the course of a year.

The math worked out to every time I bought them a meal, they purchased a house.

Billionaires, amirite?

THIRTY-ONE

Enjoy Your Money, but Spend Where You Can Make More

"I don't want to die the richest man in the cemetery."

That's what my grandfather would always tell me. His message was that while it's important to earn, he didn't want to be a slave to his profession. I see this all the time in my business. Some of my peers make a ton of coin, but they're working 24-7. They're taking calls right before they walk down the aisle at their own weddings or seconds before they give birth. You're not providing a better life for your family if you're too wrapped up in earning commission to be present for those important moments.

Being the billionaire requires balance.

My advice is that you enjoy your career but be careful that it doesn't control you. You're allowed to enjoy your money, just be smart about how you spend it. What's funny about me is that I wouldn't blink at paying $2,000 a night for a suite in a hotel, but I will lose my mind if I have to pay extra for overnight parking. I'm oddly cheap in that respect. I'll walk two blocks to park at a meter, rather than shell out $20 for a valet. I rationalize that because I pay attention to the pennies, the dollars take care of themselves.

Whatever you earn, set aside enough that you can reinvest 25 to 30 percent in whatever you need to grow your business. You're never going to be the billionaire if you don't reinvest in yourself. In my case, I spend on staffing, advertising, and marketing.

For a different profession, you may need to take professional development courses or buy more inventory or build out infrastructure. Regardless of your specific sales job, you can't grow if you're not willing to use some of what you've earned to scale up.

That said, it's important that you also enjoy your money, because you can't take it with you.

FLAGG THIS

What does "be the billionaire" mean to you? How can you apply the concept to your daily life?

PART FIVE

///

When to Say No

In the beginning of your career, you're often forced to take every opportunity that comes your way. But as I've grown as a broker, I find there's nothing worse than someone who brings bad energy to the table. Thank you, next.

It's not just about liking your client, either. Some of them have unrealistic expectations. You might be presented with the most beautiful property on the market, but if the seller isn't rational about the price, it's not worth your time. Knowing that sweet spot and managing expectations is part of the game. Sometimes that means turning down a listing you'd love to sell to free yourself up to move on to the next one.

THIRTY-TWO

///

Nancy Reagan Made It Sound So Easy, Right?

Mistakes happen, especially when you're inexperienced. My advice is, if you're going to make a huge error, do it early in your career, so you can spend the rest of your professional life learning from it.

In 2006, I was determined to get a listing on a particular house in Beverly Hills. I was twenty-two years old and beside myself with excitement about the prospect of selling a $10 million property. But the seller wasn't convinced about using me as his listing agent. In my zeal (read: greed) to get his business, I allowed myself to be reckless.

The seller was developing lots in an area I call the asshole of Palm Springs. (You'd think there were no bad investments in burgeoning Palm Springs, but *you would be wrong*.) The seller roped me in. While he didn't specifically say I could get his $10 million listing if I also invested in his Palm Springs property, he implied it.

Hello, ten million waving red flags.

Part of me understood that a deal should never be a quid pro quo because that's not a sale, it's a trade. I'm not a fur trapper in 1814; I don't exchange beaver pelts for lard. No one should have to "front" anything to get the business, especially in real estate. The only skin in the game I should have had was my time, effort, and creativity. I'm sure I knew this on some level but didn't fully accept it. I didn't listen to my instincts; I was full steam ahead.

Again, *reckless*.

The worst part is, I convinced my family to put almost $400,000 into this slippery bastard's Palm Springs property. I said this would be a fantastic investment, and because they trusted me (stupidly), they didn't do their usual due diligence, as they left this decision to the professional—me. Morons!

Turns out, the investment was worth one-twentieth of what I talked my family into paying. And because the $10 million Beverly Hills property was actually more like a $6 million house, the seller eventually took away the listing when our agreement expired because no one was willing to overpay for it.

Karma being what it is, within a few years, the seller crashed and burned because of his poor business dealings, but that was little comfort to a family out $400,000. My dad was not amused. The lesson I learned was the cost equivalent of an Ivy League undergrad *and* graduate degree, and I vowed to never screw up like that again. Fortunately, my parents ended up donating the property to charity, so at least a little good came out of it. When my dad brings it up to me I say, "Look at it this way, I didn't go to USC—or any college for that matter—so it was a wash."

Now, let's unpack what went wrong here.

The short answer is, I should have heeded Nancy Reagan's advice and just said no, early and often. While the seller wasn't totally ethical, the fault is *all mine*. I messed up.

The biggest issue is, I volunteered to invest in the Palm Springs property; I wasn't forced. I saw he was vacillating about me, and I came up with that solution to seal the deal. This is completely on me. If I met him today, I'd walk in and say, "No. I'm not buying anything. Just give me the listing. No one else is going to sell this but me," and I'd have the track record to prove it. But I didn't have billions of dollars in sales back then—I was getting all my leads exclusively by knocking on doors. I was a nobody. If I knew then what I know today, let's just say I would be living in a tax-free haven somewhere in the Caribbean.

If your first instinct is to give up a piece of what you're supposed to earn—which is *your whole reason for doing the job*—you're not negotiating from a place of strength.

People ask me all the time, "How do I figure out how to dominate when I'm in a weakened position?" You're asking the wrong question. What you should be asking yourself is how you *got* to be in the position of weakness. What steps did you skip? What information did you ignore? What shortcut did you take? This is a matter of self-reflection.

In my bad example, I could argue that I was in a position of weakness because I didn't have the confidence of dozens of luxury market sales under my belt. Maybe I should have started out selling lower-priced condos and gradually built up my business from there, but that's not the path I chose. Regardless, this argument is a red herring—my youthful inexperience wasn't the true problem.

Even though I was newish, I allowed myself to bypass the step of coming in with a compelling argument on comps. He and I never started with a realistic selling point on the (not) $10 million property. If I had convinced him to list at a market-supported, more reasonable price, he might not have hired me, and *that would have been far better for both of us in the long run.*

Months later, after his property sat stale on the market, it's likely he'd have come back to me, embracing the lower price point and setting us both up for success. At the very least, this would have spared me from some awkward conversations at Thanksgiving that year.

I ignored the step of finding information on the property in Palm Springs too. I didn't dig in. I didn't do my research. I didn't closely examine the comps out there either. I didn't talk to other brokers in the area to find out the story about his development. If I'd bothered to call one Palm Springs realtor, their laughter on the other end of the phone might have clued me in to what a bad deal these poorly located properties were.

Not only would I have known to not convince my parents to invest, but I'd also have likely taken a big step backward and reassessed if I even *wanted* to do business with a guy who was so bad it. My shortcut was simply having my family write a check instead of walking away from the deal entirely.

I approached the whole deal from a place of yes, when I should have come armed with the power of no.

Given the time, effort, and resources I used to get nowhere with the original seller, I could have listed and sold a few properties that weren't quite so unattainable. Selling four $2.5 million homes would have netted me the same returns, and it would have been easy too.

Instead, I crossed my fingers and hoped I'd get lucky.

Granted, I will admit this laissez-faire way of doing things does come with growing up around wealth, but it's no excuse. I should have been intelligent enough to know I was being stupid. That's not my parents' fault; that's my attitude on life that I am unstoppable . . . the same attitude that has taken me to the top but can also take someone to the bottom.

While success in dealmaking can come from a fortuitous break, that's not a permanent solution or a long-term strategy. A pro golfer doesn't sink a putt because of the benefit of a rogue wind one day on the links. He or she nails it because of years' practice. The golfer builds the foundation for success by constantly drilling on the fundamentals.

In the same respect, to have a successful negotiation, you must build your foundation so you're always coming from a position of strength. Work on your fundamentals: know the market, memorize the comps, be confident in what you bring to the table.

This last factor is key.

If you aren't positive that you're worth that 2.5 percent commission, if you don't believe that is your inherent value, then no one else will either. (BTW, I have no respect for cut-rate brokers—there are those who'll start off by slashing their earnings to 1 percent, or even .5 percent. Working with them, you'll definitely get what you pay for. If you're one of those people . . . you suck. Stop giving high-end brokers a bad name and making us fight for our commissions.)

That said, there may be times in your career when giving up a small portion of your earnings is the only way to get to escrow when buyers and sellers can't bridge a small gap.

Given the choice, I'd rather cede $10,000 and make $60,000 on a listing when I would have made $70,000 rather than lose the sale altogether.

Not saying no or offering a trade/discounting your services right off the bat—thus devaluing your worth—may be the biggest mistake you'll ever make.

FLAGG THIS

It's okay to get it wrong. Mistakes happen to the best of us. But if you find you're making the same mistakes over and over, ask yourself:

What steps did I skip?

What information did I ignore?

What shortcuts did I take?

How can practicing the fundamentals prevent me from ever finding myself in this position again?

Why didn't I just say no?

The Palm Springs experience taught me that sometimes it's in my best interest to turn down business. I do it all the time, and always with good reason. Later today I'm likely going to say no to Jayla after I take one more look at the comps. She said there were some off-market sales that support her price, but I'm not sure how credible she is—those numbers sound made up. Still, I owe it to myself to find out for sure. Proof won't make me more excited about her home, but it might nudge the needle enough to reconsider.

Before I go on, I must mention that I won't sign a contract with a potential buyer; that's just a deal breaker for me. While some brokers require them, I think they're offensive. I'm not an indentured servant. I need the ability to simply walk away if the relationship doesn't work. And if I'm a client, I'm not inking a contract that forces someone to stay with me for the duration, like a slave. It's ludicrous. A relationship only functions when it's mutually beneficial, and a contract won't do any-thing to fix a relationship that's gone off the rails. (The process is different with my listings, however. These are bound by a listing agreement for a set amount of time, as these can entail thousands of dollars of marketing costs.)

Sometimes, even when a property thrills me, I'll reject a client. For example, a few weeks ago I went on a listing appointment. Walking through the home, I did my whole ballet. I absolutely loved the property—it was right in my wheelhouse. It wasn't until we sat down that she said, "Yeah, I got a call the other day from a certain lottery. I talked to my son, and he said, 'It's a scam, Mom,' but I think he's wrong because they're coming Tuesday to give me a big check. Maybe it's fake, but if it isn't, I'll be in the market to buy and sell."

Ma'am, while there's a tiny chance it's real, there's an overwhelming possibility they just made an appointment to come to rob you.

In fact, why don't you put a blinking neon light over your front door that says, "Please come in and rob me and break my kneecaps"?

As I don't have time for delusion, I got the hell out of there.

Generally, I'll reject anyone who says, "I want my price and I know what I have, and somebody is going to walk in the door and give it to me. I can afford to wait."

(This reminds me of a few weeks ago when I went over to Pat Boone's house. I said, "Pat, how much do you want for the house?" He gave me a number and I said, "Pat, that seems a little steep." He then went on to tell me that Jesus wanted him to get that number and not accept a penny less. I replied, "Well, Mr. Boone, that's because Jesus was a carpenter, not a realtor.")

Two things to note here:

1. They're not listening to me or the market data on comps, so the likelihood of someone giving them that price is nil.
2. They may be able to wait, but I can't afford to waste my time with them.

I'm also super wary when a new client's first inclination is to try to get me to drop my commission. The standard commission is 5 percent, 2.5 percent to each side. The other day, I was talking to a potential buyer about a lease. (Again, leasing can lead to a large sale, if you're savvy.) In this case, said client wanted to lease a house for $10,000 per month, which is $120,000 for the year. That 5 percent commission divided by two agents comes out to $3,000 apiece. And I could potentially have to do the same amount of work as a multimillion-dollar sale, but again, loyal leasing clients have resulted in several large sales for me, so it wasn't a no right out of the gate.

Anyway, the woman I was talking to starts to get aggressive with my split—she's literally arguing with me over $3,000. I have shoes that cost more than that. I thought to myself, "I don't even know why I'm sitting here; this is a joke."

So what did I do?

I spun on the heel of my very expensive shoes and walked away from her. I also told her to go fuck herself.

Next.

THIRTY-THREE

Draw the Line . . . Even When It Hurts

There are times I won't take a listing, despite my love for the property. I hate to cede the commission, but sometimes no is the best and only answer.

For instance, I went to a potential listing on St. Ives, which is up in the ultradesirable Bird Streets in the Hollywood Hills. Everything about the property I saw was a win, from the infinity pool to the views of the Los Angeles Basin to the mature olive trees. When you think of moneyed Los Angeles, this is the home you would imagine, with all the glass walls and decadent finishes. It was perfection.

Everything went well during the appointment—I did my thing, and the homeowner was duly impressed. But there was one catch. The owner told me, "Well, I'm going to give you my business, but I need you to show that you're invested in me." I assumed this meant she wanted approval on marketing materials or maybe needed to see a PowerPoint on how we'd target potential buyers. Totally acceptable asks. But for a second, I thought she was going to propose I have sex with her, and how awkward would that be? Nope.

She said, "I want you to fix my computer. I want you to pay for it. It's $2,000."

I'm sorry, what? I believe I had a little piece of something stuck in my ear and didn't hear you.

There are a lot of out-of-pocket expenses I can justify in the listing process. I'm not afraid to kick in for a small capital improvement that would make the house more marketable. I'm all about taking sellers out to an extravagant dinner to discuss strategy. That's just the cost of doing business and something I factor into my monthly budget. Write-offs exist for a reason.

What bothered me was the temerity of the request. I didn't break her computer; I had nothing to do with her computer. Having a functional computer was not necessary for me to sell her house. And why the hell was the repair $2,000 when she could buy a brand new 24" iMac for less than $1,500? Why did I need to prove anything to her when I had more than $2 billion in sales under my belt?

Her ask was outrageous, and I hated that she wedged me into a situation where I was forced to entertain it. Ironically, while sex was off the table, she was absolutely trying to screw me.

Time and again during our sales careers, we make judgement calls on behaviors we will and will not accept from our clients. Maybe you're a young woman and you tolerate that certain month-away-from-retirement male purchasing manager who never #metoo'd you but does call you "honey." (I had a lot of weird old guys trying to kiss me on the cheek when I was an intern; best believe I constantly reassessed if the experience was worth it.) Or perhaps you're willing to be stuck listening to a high-dollar loyal client drone on about a fringe political opinion, while you arrange your gritted teeth into a semblance of a polite smile over your poached salmon lunch.

For those of us who negotiate for a living, we're often confronted with a gray area on what we're okay with and we must ask ourselves, "Do I give in and get the deal, or do I stand up for myself and leave? What's more important—the sale or my sanity?"

Knowing when and where to draw the line is a crucial part of the dealmaker's mindset.

In this case of the computer lady, I said no.

I did not take the listing. Further, I may or may not have told the homeowner what I honestly thought of her, up there in her gorgeous home, trolling desperate realtors for cash and prizes. Every instinct I had said *run*, which is why I did.

Did I make the right choice?

Of course.

Did I regret that choice when I found out that whack-a-doodle got someone else to pay to fix her computer and that broker sold her property in an eight-figure deal?

Of course.

Yet if I were confronted with that choice again, I'd make the same decision. Because I am no one's dancing monkey.

FLAGG THIS

What questionable boundaries have your clients attempted to cross?

How have you reacted?

What is a dealbreaker for you and at what point do you walk away?

—— /// ——

THIRTY-FOUR

Gatekeeping Is Another Way to Say No

Claire and I are heading into the house when my phone rings. I answer it—just like I promise everyone I'll do—and in about five seconds, I assess that this is a bogus call, not worth my time or effort. Argh.

The downside of making myself so accessible is that . . . I'm so accessible. Every day, I receive calls from people all over the country, looking for advice, hoping to pick my brain, theoretically wanting to buy property, and so on. I also get fourteen calls a day from the local penitentiary from a gentleman named Floyd who wants to marry me, but that's an entirely different story.

Very few of these are legitimate sales leads for me, because I suspect people have a lot of time on their hands. The nature of reality television leads certain viewers to imagine a connection between us. Even though I've never met them, they feel they know me. Once someone sees behind the scenes of my family, my home, my whole wedding, it cracks a window for weirdos to climb in. I will say some of them are rather entertaining, Floyd included.

In the thirty seconds I'm willing to entertain whoever is calling, I'm Googling them to see if they're legitimate. My favorite is when they start the conversation with, "You know, I don't watch the show," and then by the end of the call they're asking me, "Are you and Josh Altman really friends or enemies?" If/when they don't check out, I'm polite but direct. I ask them what I can do for them. The almost constant refrain is, "I don't want to get into it on the phone; let's meet in person for lunch." Um, yeah, file that under: *Going to Happen, Never.* Not breaking bread with a potential John Wayne Gacy, thanks.

(When I don't end up dead behind a dumpster, this is why.)

So I ask this person what I can do for them, and I get the usual answer of an in-person meeting. With unfailing politeness, I reply, "No problem! When you're ready to discuss your interests, feel free to call me back."

The usual way to shut down the weirdo, however, is to just say, "We require a financial statement before working with you." That weeds them out. Now, folks, I am not suggesting you do this, but when you are on a TV show, you must take more precautions than most people do. If you want to know if a guy is financially qualified but you don't want to sound like a jerk and ask the client for a financial statement, just say that before you start looking at houses, the agents of the listings you are going to look at like to see a proof of funds. So if they could provide a bank letter or a proof of funds—or at least a link to their company or a bio on them—that would be great. FYI, if they refuse to give you something, and you can't even Google them, they are likely fake.

Anyway, if a call is bogus, I hang up. Often, I'll block the number. This person had one shot and they biffed it.

What's a shame is, some callers do have something that I desperately need. Maybe the issue is that their product or service is a complicated solution, and they can't summarize on the phone, hence the in-person request. But I can already tell I'll be bored by someone who cannot get to the crux of it quickly.

The fact is, even the most labyrinthine ideas can be boiled down to a line or two. For example, the logline to all three action-packed hours of the movie *The Godfather* is: "The aging patriarch of an organized crime family transfers control of his clandestine empire to his son." Listen, if Francis Ford Coppola can summarize a cinematic masterpiece in a single sentence, you can do the same for the HR software you're selling.

The main problem with my unsolicited callers is that instead of immediately establishing a rapport, demonstrating we're in the same tribe, or briefly explaining why the conversation will benefit me, people try to lure me to lunch in their metaphorical (I hope) panel van with promises of puppies and jellybeans.

Many internal sales teams are rated on the metrics of their outbound dials. This is boiler-room thinking, a spray-and-pray mentality, and the mark of amateurs. If you're forced to do this at your job, you probably work for a terrible company; start applying elsewhere. That your bosses are more concerned with *quantity* over the *quality* of your interchanges tells me your company is selling something overpriced, commoditized, and useless. Kind of like a cult . . . sell you a bill of goods and then just take your money.

Seriously. Work on your résumé. You can do better.

Instead of making sixty awkward, unqualified calls in an hour, you would see far more success if you took time to qualify your leads. Figure out who's who on the org chart before dialing. Consider the title of the person you're hoping to pitch. *Be logical.* As president of The Josh Flagg Group of Companies and chairman of The Josh Flagg Foundation, do I seem like the most appropriate person to hear a pitch on printer toner?

I honestly don't like to have to say no, but I will in a minute if it costs me time. Learning to not waste your own—or your potential buyers'—time on the phone will cut down on the no's you get and will aid your pursuit of that billionaire mindset. I can't tell you how many times I stayed on the phone for ten minutes too long and wished I had that ten minutes of my life back again.

FLAGG THIS

Practice creating phone pitches to get meetings with specific people, such as a friend of your Aunt Nancy, a fellow college alum, and a guy whose LinkedIn picture shows him rock climbing.

How can you make each meeting request entice the person you're hoping to pitch? How do you establish rapport?

In what way can you demonstrate you're tribe members?

How can meeting with you help them?

Then, take a step back—is phone the best way to be in contact?

What are other creative ways you could get everyone's attention without smiling and dialing?

The other half of this equation is, what will people see if they're interested enough to google you?

Before you pitch anyone, clean up your social media or make those profiles private. Let your online presence reinforce the image you want.

———— *///* ————

THIRTY-FIVE

When No Becomes Yes

Early in my career, I was approached by a woman named Candy (not Spelling) who was looking for a summer rental by the beach. I didn't want to work with her because I didn't yet know that rental properties could be worth my time, but I literally had nothing better to do. I helped her by default.

Grudgingly, I assisted Candy in finding a rental for $40,000/month and my commission on that deal was negligible. But because I acted more enthusiastic than I felt, she and I established a solid relationship. Turns out, someone who can drop $120,000 on a summer rental should be someone I want to know. Even though I'd been hesitant to work with her at first, I made sure to keep in touch with her.

The next summer, she came around again with the same request for a summer rental. Only this time, I really threw myself into my search, and I found her a home she really loved. Because I had nothing to lose, I asked her, "Why not rent it for the entire year? That way, you can access it any time." She agreed, and that's what she did.

My wheels started turning. I figured that if she could pay almost $500,000 a year on rent, she could certainly afford to *buy* that second home, instead of just leasing it. I filed this info away in my head.

After the year passed, she wanted to rent the home for another year. Ever the opportunist, I said to her, "Why are you spending so much on rent when you could just own this place? Spending what you're spending, you could have paid for a $10 million home in ten years."

She looked at me like I'd suddenly started speaking in tongues and then she laughed and said, "Josh, I literally never thought about it before."

While she didn't buy the rental home in question, she ended up buying a $7 million house from me . . . and then she got bored with it and decided she'd rather have a place with a view. So, I resold the first one for her and got her into a $10 million home.

I like to say you can't make something out of nothing, but *something* always turns into something. In this case, a $40,000 rental turned into $24 million in sales.

Now when I work with someone on a rental, I try to be a bit of a fortune-teller, seeing into the future. In the beginning, I didn't realize the unlimited potential rentals could offer. I'm so glad that I didn't refuse her initially. Agreeing to work with her afforded me the chance to take her temperature about a bigger deal down the road.

Will there always be people out to waste my time, especially when it comes to a rental property?

God, yes.

But being a pro means that I'm able to sniff out fakers quickly. As the leasing agent, it's not always appropriate for me to ask them for a financial statement before I take them out, as that's up to the landlord/owner. I'm offering up my time and contacts in good faith. I try to feel potential leasers out in a nonoffensive way.

If the renter isn't forthcoming and I'm really struggling to figure out if they're genuinely able to afford the place, I'll blame the owner's agent, saying, "I would so love to show you this home, but the other agent is being a stickler. They need me to show them you're the real deal, which obviously you are. I hope you're not mad, but it's protocol."

A common retort to this argument is, "We're very private people."

Wrong answer.

There's *always* documentation. If you're in the market to drop a half mil per year on a rental property, someone has written an article about you. You exist in the public record. Fact.

Bottom line, if the renters still fight being vetted after all this, it's a no for me, dawg. Lots of people out there will take advantage of agents' time and largess, but I refuse to be one of them.

Still, I find it's often worth it to help people looking for a lease . . . especially when I know that a little bit of effort now can lead to a $600,000 commission check later: I'm never too busy to cash one of those.

Sometimes what feels like it should be a no turns into a yes after a bit of reflection and research.

Learning to discern between them is money in the bank.

PART SIX

///

Know the Playing Field

I know more about the history of luxury real estate in Beverly Hills than anyone else I've ever met, thanks to the foundation of those early ten thousand hours. If someone has bought or sold a home in the 90210, I can tell you who, when, and how much. Knowing the market is the savviest way to show your value as a dealmaker. The more knowledgeable you are about the trivial details, the more your clients will trust and defer to you for the large details.

I can tell you what someone paid for their house, who lives there, how many square feet they have, how big the property is, what they owe on the house and essentially their social security number . . . there is nothing I don't know. Trust me when I go up for that listing appointment, I get that shit because I know more than anyone . . . well, that or they call the police because they think I am a stalker. Frankly, most times people are just blown away and they say I am an idiot savant to which I respond with, "No, just an idiot."

High-end property clients are intelligent—they typically run their own businesses, manage global accounts, or have some sort of influence in the world. They're detail oriented and don't suffer fools gladly. Yet, they don't always default to rational factors when choosing a home, so it's essential you know your stuff, paying close attention to the logical and emotional factors at play. Because that's when you truly bring your clients a one-of-a-kind experience.

THIRTY-SIX

Know Your Shit

I can't state this enough—know your shit. While you can set yourself apart from most of your peers by being the most polished, the most professional, the most proactive, if you aren't also the most well versed in your product/your vertical/your service/your cause, none of the above matters. Your new lip injections won't inspire confidence (especially if you can see them on your own face without looking in a mirror) if you don't back that big beak up with an innate understanding of every deal that's closed within ten square miles.

In my business, knowing my shit means that I'm practically omniscient about the market, and I have an unquenchable thirst to learn more. I can't rest on my laurels, because the marketplace is dynamic and ever changing. Real estate news is always breaking news. If a house just sold above or below ask, I'll find out why. If a perfectly good property at a perfectly reasonable price has been sitting, I'll get the skinny. My business thrives on rumor, so my ear is never not to the ground. This helps set me apart from the competition.

I cannot overstate why I must possess a firm grasp on every aspect of buying and selling in Los Angeles. I am my clients' greatest asset, so it's my professional responsibility to retain an encyclopedic knowledge to use for their benefit.

Let's discuss a property on Montcalm as an example of how I use my extensive knowledge to sell. First, as a native Angeleno, I'm an expert regarding the various neighborhoods. The geography is easy because I've been driving these streets since I was sixteen and touring them since my days of refusing naps. You want the best route from A to Z? I'm your guy. And I can detail the topography, from rivers to lakes to mountains to woods. You may as well call me Google maps.

Beyond that, I'm familiar with the nuances that give each neighborhood its distinct personality. Wanna live all your best midcentury modern life in what feels like a Richard Neutra or Pierre Koenig fever dream? I can show you ten perfect homes.

Or would you rather be around other families who eschew razors and brew their own kombucha but also can't survive without their Viking appliances? I got you, boo.

Care to settle in an abode that's so high up you need supplemental oxygen? I know just the place.

Or would you prefer the safety of the one area where coyotes won't eat your purse dog? I'm all over it.

What all this means is, I could describe in detail all the local color before I ever drove through the gates at the home on Montcalm.

The Montcalm estate was a bit of a unicorn, as it's located in the eastern portion of Hollywood on a rare seven-acre plot. (In this part of the city, you're more likely to stumble across someone with their original nose/cup size/hairline than this much contiguous land.) Given the acreage, the views, and the proximity to Mulholland Drive, I was already calculating prices before I even stepped inside the home. Cha-ching!

This home would be a slam dunk for a developer, right?

Wrong!

The homeowner's preference was that the buyer would appreciate and preserve this historical home, so the onus was on me to learn all about the property's intricacies so I could sell to *that* person. The process entailed familiarizing myself far beyond the specs and square footage. I needed to dig deep on how this home would emotionally resonate with a history-positive potential buyer.

My favorite properties have a story and the home on Montcalm did not disappoint. This Spanish-style villa had been built in the 1920s and lovingly preserved since then. So many of the original details were still there, from the colorful tiles embossed with fire-breathing dragons to the Prohibition-era secret wine cellar. I love catering to buyers who are equally obsessed with Old Hollywood, and I knew this house would resonate with them. Those buyers would swoon over hearing about how the home had been owned first by a silent film star and then by the Oscar-winning composer of *Ben-Hur*.

So I learned everything I could about not only who lived there previously, but *how* they lived. One of the former residents used to host huge parties and his raucous guests—including Charlie Chaplin—would autograph the walls of the secret wine cellar.

To properly sell this house, I had to delve further into my interests in design and architecture so I could fully describe the features the less thorough might miss.

Spoiler alert: it's never a chore when it's already something I love to do.

Before I show any house, I learn both when and why the house was built, as the whys are often compelling. What might seem like a design flaw, like the case of the not-easily accessible wine cellar, becomes fascinating when given the context of the era. Understanding the provenance is also important. While one might be quick to dismiss what looks like weird, dated Renaissance Faire–style tiling, they're suddenly a unique selling point upon learning they were hand-painted by Franciscan monks.

I hated hearing that some brokers came through and *apologized* to potential buyers about the staircase, touting how easily a skilled contractor could change it. That certainly wasn't my approach. Instead, I leaned into those funky stairs as a feature. While the wrought iron spiral staircase wasn't everyone's taste, potential buyers quickly warmed to them upon hearing about how they were modeled after the Tulip stairs in the Queen's House in London. The line between "homely" and "historical" can be a thin one, so I make sure I position myself on the right side.

Of course, I'll always know the basics, like how and when the home might have been renovated, any natural disasters that might have affected the home, and any criminal activity including mass murder or suicides. It's also important to disclose if the home is on the sight of an ancient burial ground. (Listen, we all saw *Poltergeist*.) While legally obligated to disclose this information, that doesn't mean these data points are hindrances. For example, with the advent of true crime podcasts, former crime scenes can be a hot commodity (you beautiful psychopaths).

After I'd gotten the listing, I suggested the Montcalm executors make a handful of renovations to reinforce the notion that the home had been well maintained. With a few coats of paint and fresh landscaping, the home suddenly had the curb appeal it had lacked. First impressions count. If a buyer doesn't have a positive vibe when pulling up to the home, it will color their whole perspective.

Bottom line, instead of doing the necessary deep historical dive, other brokers blathered on about this home's potential for redevelopment when they showed it and they didn't get any offers. But I knew that if I found the right buyers, they would fall in love with what made it unique and historical, preserving the executor's vision, and that's exactly what happened.

When the Montcalm house sold, even though it took a bit more effort on my part, it broke records for sale price in that neighborhood . . . all because I knew my shit.

FLAGG THIS

What are ten different ways you can better educate yourself on your product, your market, and your competitors?

Where do you find the information?

What contacts must you make?

Once you determine these ways, how will you use them to enhance your current pitch?

THIRTY-SEVEN

Don't Keep It to Yourself

Now, what goes hand in hand with knowing your shit?
Making sure everyone else knows you know it too.

I sold a beautiful Spanish style house in the flats of Beverly Hills. It was just gorgeous and fully appointed with radiantly lit landscaping—your garden variety Beverly Hills flats home. The place was special, but I had to find a way to make it *special* because no one's going to write about how I sold yet another lovely home in a neighborhood full of lovely homes.

Where's the story?

What's the angle?

Who cares?

Well, I care, because I'm perpetually looking for ways to promote myself. I'm always on the hunt for an angle to publish. To be successful in this business, it's not enough to make the sales—I must publicize them too. It's the whole tree-falling-in-the-forest analogy and creating an Ouroboros of sales leading to publicity leading to sales leading to publicity and so on for infinity. (If you didn't Google it, an Ouroboros is a snake swallowing its own tail. You're welcome.)

Anyway, I searched the public records. I found out that the house was once owned by Ruth Chatterton, a 1920s starlet. That's all I needed to know. I immediately called up Ruth Ryon, the former celebrity real estate columnist for the *L.A. Times*. Before she retired, she spent twenty-three years writing the *Hot Properties* column. (RIP, Ruth Ryon.) I said, "Ruth, you've got to put this house in *Hot Properties*. Ruth Chatterton owned it!"

She replied, "Who the fuck is Ruth Chatterton?"

Instead of saying, "Um, she's some lady I found on IMDb," I *sold* her on Chatterton.

I said, "Ruthie, don't you know who Ruth Chatterton is? Google it. Oh, my God. She was the biggest starlet of the twenties!" That is, until the talkies ruined her career!

The reality is, Chatteron once owned the house in the 1960s, and I didn't do a full biography on her life, but I didn't need to in order to get Ryon excited about idea.

All I needed was the angle.

I've said it before, but in this town, people are always seeking brushes with fame, and I use that to my advantage. For purposes of the article, Chatteron was like Norma Desmond for *Sunset Boulevard*, huge mega star of the 1920s. The true details didn't matter because Ruth got an interesting article about it, and I had my sale publicized.

Only later did I find out what a fascinating woman Chatterton was. She got her start after she criticized a play she'd seen. Her friend told her she should try being an actress if she could do it so much better . . . so she did. I love that. Later in her career, she was nominated for an Academy Award for Best Actress. She went on to become a bestselling novelist and one of the first female aviators and good friend to Amelia Earhart.

If I ever get the chance to resell this house, you can bet I'll capitalize on Chatterton's *full* history.

—— /// ——

The Art of Storytelling

So much of sales is understanding how to tell a story, such as I did with Ruth Chatterton. One of the reasons Edith was so successful is because she embraced the power of storytelling, even if whatever happened to her wasn't that amusing or profound in the moment.

The power comes from the retelling.

The *selling* comes from the retelling.

The other day, I said to someone, "I'm telling you a story now that is going to sound amazing. But I promise you when it happened in real life, it wasn't that great."

What happened was, Edith and my grandfather Eric were sitting in a bar in the South of France when two sex workers approached them. One sits next to Edith, the other sits next to Eric. My grandmother was born without a filter, so there was nothing she wouldn't ask and no one she wouldn't grill. She turns to one woman and asks, "What do you charge per night?"

The woman replies, "I charge 700 francs."

Edith nods, digesting this information, likely calculating how that broke down on a per-minute basis. Then my grandfather turns to the woman at his side and asks, "Well, what are you charging per night?"

The second woman replies, "I charge 1,200 francs."

This disparity bothered Edith greatly. Why not equal pay for equal work? So Edith asks them both, "Why do you cost 700 francs when she gets 1,200?"

The 1,200-franc sex worker replies, "Because I have a college education."

Now, I promise the story didn't unfold as funny as that. It was probably more like, "I don't know, maybe because I'm smarter than her." In fact, the way it really happened was, they probably didn't even respond. Likely, my grandparents overheard them talking about their rates; but who cares, it makes for an amazing story!

The point is, it's always about the story *and* how you're able to tell it. In the version where one insults the other's intelligence, it seems kind of sad. But when told with my grandmother's slant, it comes across entirely different, charming, and more empowered. It also helped that she was a five-foot-tall woman with broken English, which just makes everything that much more amusing.

Everyone has a story, but the best salespeople understand how to use a story to their advantage.

THIRTY-NINE

Brokers' Price Opinion

What do you think the first thing I do is when I get a new listing?
Come up with a clever backstory?

Stage the home?

Create marketing material?

Place an ad?

None of the above.

The very first thing I do is visit the neighbors.

In high-end neighborhoods, there's a strong possibility that the folks next door want to expand their property. So before I invest the time, dollars, and effort it takes to sell a multimillion-dollar piece of real estate, I cross my seller's lawn and knock on the neighbor's door. Even if they're not looking to expand, quite often, they have friends or family hoping to make a move to this neighborhood, and I'd never know if I didn't ask.

So many people want to complicate the process of selling a house, but successful real estate sales boil down to three factors:

1. ABP—Always Be Publicizing.
2. Show a property to its full advantage.
3. Know how to close the deal.

You don't need to throw a Burgers and Botox party, and you don't have to take a potential buyer on a helicopter ride for an aerial view of the property (even if it is chic). These three factors are the fundamentals, and they're the pathway to success.

Remember it's real estate, not rocket science.

All of this, however, is predicated on pricing the home correctly.

The harsh truth is that everyone imagines their home is worth more than it is. Doesn't matter the price point, the seller always feels they should list higher than the market will bear, no matter if it's a $700,000 condo or $30 million estate—because their home is special. And it is. *To them.*

Regardless of how good a seller's taste is, how well they're staged, how spotless their inspection, their place is almost always worth less than the best-case scenario of their imagination. This is a hard conversation to have with the homeowner. Telling a seller that the magical setting where twenty wonderful Christmases played out won't fetch as much as they'd like goes down just as well as informing a new mother her bullet-headed baby is ugly.

Doesn't matter if it's truth, no one wants to hear it. (P.S. Maybe put a hat on that kid; his cone head is freaking me out.)

My dilemma is always bringing a seller to reality, both tactfully and in a way that ensures I win the business. The seller's natural predisposition is to go with the broker who estimates the highest . . . right? Because more money validates all the happy times they had there. But unless the broker is buying the place themselves, feeding into this fairytale *does the seller no favors.*

When this happens, and it happens *a lot*, I have a way to work around it.

I'll tell the homeowner, "Look, here's the deal. I can give you exactly what you want to hear right now and walk out of here with the listing. But, at this point in my career, I'm not interested in collecting listings. I'm more concerned with getting repeat business and making people happy."

(Seriously, I am.)

I'll continue, "I need you to understand that other brokers are going to come in here, and they're going to tell you what you want to hear. If you choose to go with them, I won't stop you. Thing is, six months from now, you're just going to call me, and I'll be back again when it's time to sell the property for a smaller amount, after it's been reduced ten times. So you can do that, or you can let me just tell you what it's really worth and we'll get this closed in no time." Then that's exactly what I do.

The direct approach can get sellers to listen to reason, but sometimes it's not enough to hear it from me. Homeowners want to argue because other brokers told them more, not because they can sell at that price, but because it's the lazy way to score a listing. I run into this all the time.

Often, once a buyer signs with these (delusional) brokers, it's easier just to drop prices again and again than to find a different agent. Sure, these realtors may eventually sell the place, but they're never going to get repeat business from the seller. No one wants to work with the guy or gal who kept dragging strangers and their dirty shoes across their Berber carpeting for six months, perpetually calling with disappointing news. That's no way to build loyalty.

After my blunt assessment, I'll say, "This is what it's worth, and guess what? If you don't think that's the case, how about this—let's test out the market. Let's get twenty other agents in here that aren't trying to compete for the listing and have nothing to lose by being honest. After we sign the listing contract, I'll get them in here and we'll get their opinions as well."

I call this process the Brokers' Price Opinion. When the sellers go along with the suggestion, we always end up with a home that's priced right and sells quickly.

But if somehow the idea of soliciting the Brokers' Price Opinion doesn't resonate with the seller, and maybe it makes them think I don't know the value, I'll say, "How about this? Let's quote a higher price, like everyone else is telling you. Let's wait a month and keep this as a pocket listing. We'll see how that price resonates off the market, and we'll get feedback from potential buyers. If they don't agree with the high price you want, we'll list it at what I believe it should be."

Spoiler alert: ninety-nine times out of one hundred, the home sells for almost the exact price I've predicted.

Here's the thing—I'm basing the comp price on my entire depth and breadth of knowledge, because pricing a home is more than just measuring it against the sale price of comparable properties.

Lawrence Block, Beverly Hills' first realtor, used to say that a property was worth whatever someone is willing to pay for it. That's as true today as it was back then.

It's a given that I'm up to date on what everything sells for in my area, but that's only part of the equation. Any good broker can tell you what sold at what price, but a great broker will be privy to *why* the properties sold at that price. The *whys* can be just as important as the *how much*.

They key to finding your seller's most accurate price is to know the stories of the outliers—those homes that sold above or below the norm. For instance, the neighbors to the north might have sold their home cheaply to a friend who was bailing them out of financial trouble. The neighbors to the south might have gotten higher than what the market would bear because it was the buyer's childhood home and they wanted it at any price. It's possible the price was skewed because an equity firm like the Blackstone Group swooped in and overbid because they're bullish on the market and they wanted that property as part of their rental portfolio.

A broker's credibility depends on understanding all aspects of what goes into pricing a home. That way, I'm able to answer a seller who doesn't understand why their home isn't worth as much as the house down the street was.

When I can explain why the other buyer paid the premium my client's home won't bear, I'll save face . . . and the commission.

/ / /

FORTY

Help Me Help You (with Marketing)

If a tree fell in a forest and no one heard it, would it still make a sound?

Considering I don't traffic in trees or forests, the metaphysics regarding observation and thought is not my problem. (If you feel like taking a few bong hits and contemplating it all, be my guest.) But if I have a home for sale and no one knows? Big problem. Huge.

Part of knowing the playing field is understanding how to use marketing. That's why I have a tried and true, multifaceted approach to marketing my homes, predicated on the notion that the only thing I hate wasting more than time is money.

The short of it is, I don't sell homes; I sell dreams.

Wait, did you throw up in your mouth a bit over that terrible line? Sorry.

How about this instead? My personal credo is that I build a story and brand around each property that I represent. I liken what I do to a luxury clothier on Rodeo Drive. You wouldn't ever want to shop there by looking through a dusty old catalog of couture, right?

High-end stores create an experience. Recently, I went to Gucci in Florence, and it was as much a modern art museum as it was a clothing store. The lights, the music, the way the clothing was staged to look like an exhibit—it was all an irresistible multimedia happening that never stopped reminding me that I was in Gucci in Italy and that this crazy, Technicolor, larger than life art/fantasy fusion could be mine if I bought the pants and the belt. Everything in that store was strategically arranged to attract maximum sales while reinforcing the brand.

This is how I market homes.

I look at each property as a product, and I accomplish this in a couple ways.

First, and this is a refrain I will repeat throughout this book, I price the home via market dictates. The appropriateness of the price is directly proportional to how quickly it will sell.

The beauty of the right price is it attracts buyers. A right-priced home often results in a bidding war, which then *raises the price*. Listen, I am a greedy son of a bitch. It costs me a lot of money to look this good. I want the most from the sale, but the sale must happen for me to collect my fee. I don't want 2.5 percent of a whole lot of nothing; I want 2.5 percent of the *right* price.

When I market a property, my aim is to get a prospect to fall in love with it on his or her smartphone. I'm like the witch in Hansel and Gretel, luring kids into her gingerbread home—and subsequently, her oven—because they think it's made of candy. I create the desire to see that shit in person; you know, kick the tires. Lick the walls.

I create demand for each home as its own unique property. I'm in the business of manufacturing desire; I want each property to seem irresistible. As people view listings on social media, I play up the open houses as social events—go there, meet people, buy the home that will reinforce the image of you living your best life.

Along with the direct mail I mentioned in an earlier chapter, I also regularly advertise in the *L.A. Times*, and I make the most of each ad. I opt for the double-page, four-color spread, and it's always the most visually attractive portion of the newspaper. That is not an accident. My ads get seen and they generate interest.

While *MDLLA* is a phenomenal personal marketing tool, most houses are already sold by the time the episode airs. The benefit is the show has made me a household name in the real estate oeuvre and gives me a huge advantage over my competitors.

Since the show can't feature every client's house, I make the most of each listing by creating exciting virtual tours for properties that I share on all my social networks. I couple this effort with a concentrated effort of targeted ads on Facebook and Instagram. This allows my team to capture email addresses we use to follow up and schedule in-person tours. (After we qualify the buyers, of course. I love my fans, but I am not wasting the day taking them on a free tour. Listen, it is expensive to be me.) The social media platforms are a boon because of the metrics they provide. I can measure the engagement for each campaign and adjust accordingly.

I also employ opt-in email marketing, and I have a database of more than fifty thousand addresses for the best agents, developers, and clients, all around the globe. The minute a listing goes live, my entire network is informed.

Redundancy is key, so I also catalog all my efforts on JoshFlagg.com, which I modeled after the highest-end jewelers and hoteliers. My site gets millions of visitors each year, and it creates so much exposure for all my clients. Because I have a team that manages the site, it's dynamic and ever changing. We have the capability to quickly react and adapt to all feedback, tweaking copywriting, design, and usability in moments. Every feature is optimized.

I didn't roll out my marketing efforts all at once. I gradually introduced them, one by one, as technology and budgets dictated. The point is, you must let potential clients know that your product or services are an option. You might be the best salesperson in the world, but it won't matter if you're not getting in front of the right people.

If you're a single practitioner, look to how your competition markets themselves. Figure out your angle and follow suit. Invest in yourself and you'll reap the rewards. And if you don't have the budget, work social media until you do.

If you're backed by a corporate entity, take your knowledge of your customer base and share it with the marketing team. They work only with the information they have, so educate them to help reinforce your efforts. So often corporate teams are measured not by the quality of their material but through task completion. They exist because you're out there selling. Make them create the kind of support that works for you; you have that cache.

Every corporate team is a considered a cost center, save for the sales department. It's because of *you* that your company exists. So sales management has the power to demand better assistance from marketing. Scrutinize their efforts. Volunteer to act as a liaison between your team and theirs. The resources exist, so make sure they're helping you reach your goals.

Or your dreams. Your call.

FORTY-ONE

Create Case Studies

I'm naturally predisposed to write down what I hope to remember. I started doing this when I was fourteen years old. I wanted to create a record of Edith's stories because I knew she wouldn't be around forever. While it took a decade to complete, *A Simple Girl: Stories My Grandmother Told Me* is a first-person account of her life, and I cherish that work.

The inclination to put pen to paper has served me well in my sales career. I do so many deals that I often forget the intricacies of them. (Humblebrag.) At this point, whatever challenge is thrown at me, I've likely faced it before, so it's helpful to have documentation for quick reference. And when I forge fresh territory, I definitely want a record of what I did. That's why I recommend any dealmaker put together case studies of his or her accomplishments.

Case studies can be a powerful sales tool. They're so effective because they're detailed, up-close examinations of an issue and its resolution. I use them to provide a framework of the steps I've taken to solve a complex problem.

For example, if I work a deal with a particularly complicated financial structure with contingencies and leasebacks, I'll document the whole thing. I'll record not only all the salient details but also how my being able to creatively problem solve positively affected the buyer or seller, that is, the family was able to stay in their sold home long enough for their high school senior to graduate with his class.

When I create a case study that highlights the facts, and I infuse those facts with feelings, I'll always have an effective tool that edifies, informs, and reinforces my accomplishments, not just in sales but in any endeavor.

Whatever it is you've done, document it. Did you engineer a solution that will appeal not only to mom-and-pop shops but also applies at the enterprise level? Did your creative problem-solving save your customer thousands of dollars a year on their HR costs? Did you program a virus to knock out the mainframe on the invading aliens' spaceship and save the whole damn world on July 4? Wait, that's the plot to *Independence Day*.

Regardless, welcome to Earth . . . and write it down.

FLAGG THIS

Create a case study about a frequent problem you've solved for your client. Per author Neil Patel of neilpatel.com, here are eight tips for creating a more effective case study:

- Write about someone your ideal customer will relate to.
- Tell the story from start to finish.
- Make your case study easy to read.
- Include real numbers.
- Talk about specific strategies in your case studies.
- Test different content formats.
- Appeal to different types of learners.
- Make your case studies easy to find.

FORTY-TWO

Use Your Knowledge to Be a Trusted Advisor

M y phone buzzes and I glance at the number on my dashboard's Bluetooth display. I shudder inadvertently. I'm not looking forward to this conversation, but I must take it. While initially painful, I do my best to deal with whatever's unpleasant immediately rather than letting it fester in the hopes it goes away.

Spoiler alert: it *never* goes away.

I find it's best to deliver bad news as quickly and logically as possible; there's no other option. In these instances, I know a client will react emotionally, so the onus is on me to keep my cool and stay professional. I never shout, *"Bitch, why did you not listen?!"* although I'm often tempted. Instead, I cite facts, exactly like I know I'm about to do.

"Josh here."

The client is a seller who's refused to heed my advice. I should have never taken the listing (see: *Garbage, Don't Sell*); I did it as a favor. But the client did me no favors by flatly refusing every piece of guidance I've offered him. Instead of tapping into my years of experience and vast knowledge base, he decided to proceed as he saw fit, and now he's mad at me for his own damn choices. This is a lose-lose proposition, and the only way to keep it from escalating is to stay calm.

"Josh, why don't we have any offers?" the devil on the other end barks.

"Because we're priced too high," I explain for the hundredth time. "I have a variety of properties listed right now anywhere from $1 million to $20 million, and yours is the only one not getting any traction, out of every home I've listed. Now, why do you think that is?" (You know, when I say this to clients, I can never tell if this makes a lightbulb go off in their heads or if they're thinking to themselves that I am spending more time on my other listings and not theirs.)

This is because Lucifer here wants $3.5 million for a home where the land is worth $2 million, on its best day. His listing is dated and in desperate need of a remodel, as the finishes are from back when Britney and Justin wore matching denim to the VMAs. There's not a single thing about the home or the dirt it sits on that would merit a price within $1 million of his ask. This is not news, yet he treats it as though it were.

"The house does not sell because you are not a good agent."

My voice belies my lack of patience. "An agent doesn't bring showings; the market brings showings. Now, if the market doesn't bring showings, what do you think that means?" It means you're *fucking overpriced*. Give it back to the guy. Show him he's an idiot and has a part in this, and show him you're frustrated too. You're putting work and effort, and he is dicking around here because he is stopping you from doing your job. You've got to take that approach or he right away is going to pin *you* as the problem, not *him*. In this situation, it's imperative you beat him to the punch. I keep putting the question back on him, as ultimately, he's the cause of this dilemma.

"That means that I should fire you."

"Beelzebub, I wish you would," I think.

But we're still under contract, and it is my professional obligation to try to guide him—yet again—to making a better decision, regardless of how satisfying it would be to shout back or slap the smug off his face. Prediction? This is not going to end well. Even if I miraculously sell the place before the listing agreement ends, this guy is going to hate me regardless, so I proceed as though I have nothing to lose. Sometimes, that's the only choice.

"Here's what we know," I say. "The house needs either a major remodel or a complete teardown. I respect that you've been happy and comfortable there, as it is your home. But the reality is, it's not new or fresh, and there are no aspects about the property that will command anywhere near $3.5 million. I told you this on the first day, the first week, and the first month and the market has continued to confirm it. Everyone who's seen this place has laughed at the price. I told you it would sit at your ask and now it's sitting. None of this should be a surprise."

"I think you are not working hard enough for me."

Mephistopheles, please.

"Your property's price is working against you," I reason. "Let's be real. If you want to sell it, you must reduce your price. The market will not support your ask, not even close, as has been proven."

And now we get to the root of the problem. "But if I do that, I will not make a big profit on it."

"If you don't reduce the price now, you're going to eventually lose money. I'm giving you the benefit of my fifteen years of wisdom from this business. You. Are. Over. Priced."

"I think you should let me out of my contract."

I take a deep breath and continue to speak professionally, but it's increasingly more difficult. "I will never force anyone to stay in a contract they feel is not working for them. You are welcome to find another broker. But let me ask you this—are they going to answer the phone?"

I know I do because I talk to this guy *every day*. Hell, I wound up with him because everyone else stopped taking his calls.

He grumbles a noncommittal response.

This place will never sell and I need to cut my losses, but it's important that it's the seller's idea, not mine. I say, "Why don't we do this—if you believe so strongly in the house, why don't you stay there for a while? We can pull it off the MLS while you refinance it. Money is so cheap right now; you'll get a far better rate than what you had. Maybe once you get some breathing room, you can reconsider whether you want to live there long term or if you want to take that extra capital to remodel it to make it more appealing to a buyer. After you're refinanced, you can come back onto the market at a price the market will support, without your losing money on it."

"Hmph." There's a long pause and he finally tells me, "That sounds like a good idea."

Praise Jewish Jesus.

Now, if he'd only listened to this suggestion when I made it at the listing appointment, I could have saved us all some time and frustration, yet here we are. But I don't say any of this. Instead of a refrain from the "I Told You So" chorus, I confirm that we should remove the home from the MLS.

For the first time since I became the Devil's advocate, he sounds happy.

As I suspected, he never wanted to sell his place, and now I've given him a way out.

This situation is evidence that as hard as I try to be a trusted advisor, there are times that buyers don't listen to me. Doesn't matter how smart a purchase the property may be, people have a vision of what they want, especially when they seek a *home* and not just a sound investment. I guess it's like how some justify staying with a bad partner, all, "The heart wants what the heart wants." No one ever completes the end of that sentence with, "Because the heart is stupid," but we're all thinking it.

A few years ago, there was a home in Beverly Hills I'd seen multiple times. I brought all my buyers there because the location was ideal, and the price was right. Sure, the aesthetics were a bit dated, but its history made up for it. The previous owner had created an iconic '80s television show inside this very place. I was a sucker for knowing how that house had helped inform the way he wrote the show, and the entire culture it influenced to be more glamorous via use of oversized shoulder pads.

The property was solidly built with fine bones. The lot was full of mature landscaping and backed up to a cliff, so it was a private green enclave. It's my job to guide buyers to look past what a property is and to what it could be, and this place was rife with potential. Unfortunately, I could not convince anyone else about my vision.

I worried I was losing my touch.

The creator's home wasn't my listing, so technically, it was neither my circus nor my monkeys. But the old Jewish man inside of me couldn't stop obsessing about what a great deal it was. Meshuggeneh! The home was priced badly and represented by a putz who wasn't great at his job, so it had languished on the market for more than a year. Why wasn't anyone listening to my excellent advice? *Oy!*

I kept my eye on the place, until the price went so low that I had to do something.

I bought the damn thing myself.

I lived in that lovely home for five months before I flipped it for *$1 million more than I paid for it*. (Feel free to repeat that line with your pinky to your lip, Dr. Evil–style.) I knew it was valuable! And before you ask, nope, I didn't upgrade a thing. In fact, it was in worse condition after my few months of wear-and-tear than when I bought it. Better yet, it was my own listing, so I got a commission on the sale too.

A few years have now passed, and the home is worth a couple million more than I flipped it for. But I moved the money into a better property, so we are all good.

The moral of the story is, the depth and breadth of your knowledge is valuable, even if your buyers are too stubborn to realize it.

FLAGG THIS

Sometimes it's not you, it's them. As long as you're not selling crack, it's perfectly fine to get high on your own supply.

———— /// ————

FORTY-THREE

Son of a Sailor

I have the next couple hours of today blocked off to show properties to a developer. The developer has recently relocated to L.A. from New York, where he'd spent his career renovating properties in the Hamptons. After his divorce, his wife and child moved out here, so he followed them.

The gentleman is soft spoken and dressed for an afternoon of sailing an old teak Chris-Craft across the wind-lapped waves off Montauk. Because of that, we shall address him going forward as "the Commodore." The Commodore looks like an anachronism on the plastic streets of L.A., and I already like him because of it. Or maybe I like him because he's in the market for properties high in the hills, somewhere in the range of $10–$20 million, with the anticipation of a total tear-down and rebuild. Whatever, either way works.

Yes, I understand the idea of razing a $20 million home sounds insane—possibly even obscene—but look at it in the context that the Commodore can rebuild and resell for up to $100 million in that same spot. Land is a limited resource and the dirt he's about to see? That will more than pay for itself.

I have ten properties to show him today, and a few more tomorrow. We pull away from his luxury accommodations at the Peninsula and begin to drive down Santa Monica. Claire isn't with us, but she'll text me each time we need to leave a listing to get to the next one in time.

I quickly assess that the Commodore is the consummate businessman as we view the first home. He ignores the custom finishes and infinity edge pool as we traverse a property with 360-degree views. The air up here is clear, with a light breeze that smells like blooming jasmine. It's a slice of paradise. Even though so many of the homes we're set to see look like they could belong to a Bond villain with their soaring ceilings and vast expanses of glass, his only interest is in how much land there is and how much earth will need to be leveled and stabilized to create more flat surfaces for building. He has zero emotion about the potential transaction. The property's historical context is of no interest, so I don't bring any details up while we're on site, saving the interesting Hollywood Regency–era info for the places we pass as we move from one appointment to the next.

The Commodore's into collecting classic cars, as well as boats, so we trade stories about the love/hate relationships we have with our vehicles. He pulls out a photo of a car he saw and liked today, and I have to laugh—it belongs to my friend Roxy. And with that, the Commodore recognizes that we're in the same tribe and I'm worthy of his trust.

He tells me his father was in the same business and was famous for saying, "Would you buy it for a dollar? If your answer is yes, then it all comes down to a question of price." I like that philosophy.

We pull up to a Spanish style home with a generous parking pad and large backyard, listed at $14 million, or, what we call in Los Angeles, midpriced. The agent isn't there yet, so we walk around back to see the views. While the home isn't perfect for the Commodore's purposes, it could work. He'd definitely buy it for a dollar, so where he'd go from there is subject to negotiation.

We wait out front for the agent to arrive, and the Commodore does some back-of-the-envelope math, taking the price per square foot and factoring in materials and labor, plus the million-dollar architect's fee, as there's only a handful of them in Los Angeles who specialize in creating builds for this kind of lot.

When someone finally pulls up, it's a twenty-something young man in a battered Chevy Malibu with a Legalize It bumper sticker. (FYI, weed has been legal here since 2016.) He exits the vehicle in paint-splattered clothing, informing us the broker sent him to let us in.

I try not to judge a book by its cover, so I ask Mr. Bumper Sticker some questions. Maybe he's an artist and I should be buying his work? However, he can't answer any of them, shrugging and telling us, "Sorry, brah, I'm just the dude with the keys."

Next.

We look at a home on the same street where I recently sold Matthew Perry's house. We're greeted by yet another assistant, this time young and female and likely biding her time until she's cast on *Love Island*. She has no idea of the property's square footage and seems more interested in playing with the homeowner's assorted small dogs than showing us the property. "Just, like, look around or whatever," she tells us as she buries her face in the snarling Pomeranian's ample neck fur.

We start outside. The views are spectacular and the whole city is visible, but the Commodore is concerned about the lot size. This home would work only if he could buy the place next door, too. Was that an option? Dog Lover does not know any specifics about the neighbors when asked, although she can tell us all their pets' names.

Our afternoon progresses. We see some places of interest, but there are no adults on site anywhere. In one home with a massive green rolling lawn backed up to Bel Air Country Club, we're greeted not by an agent but by a group of influencers having a photo shoot for custom hair extensions. They are delighted to meet me, and we pose for a group photo. While it's cute, I'd have preferred someone there to answer questions other than which faux ponytail might best work for my current style.

Out of the nine homes we've seen, not one of them has had an agent on site. At this point, I'm embarrassed. Not for me, and not for the properties I'm showing, as several of them are appropriate for the Commodore's purposes. I'm appalled by the lack of respect these brokers have for their high-value clients. Would any of these sellers have listed with them if the brokers had been honest about who'd show the property?

While the market is red-hot right now, housing sales are cyclical, and signs point to a potential upcoming slump. These other brokers should be jumping at the chance to meet a high-net-worth developer, if for no reason other than to talk to him about their pocket listings.

Am I the only person who likes money??

Miraculously, an agent is there to greet us at the last listing. The property is the most level we've seen and comes with the best views. The seller is looking for $17 million but is willing to consider any compelling offer.

Guess what? This is good information to share if you'd like to sell a home.

After a few quick calculations based on the numbers the onsite broker is there to provide, the Commodore can determine that he'd happily pay up to $14 million for this place. We'll write the offer for less, but I don't anticipate many problems with getting this for his ask.

For all the effort and the hustling, sometimes it can feel too easy. But don't forget the years of work and study it took me to winnow down all the properties that the Commodore would want. Our successful encounter didn't occur in a vacuum or without extensive history.

Our experience today makes me think of the old Italian proverb about a man who's in desperate financial straits. Every day, he goes to the town square to pray to the statue of a saint in its center. He gets down on his knees daily and begs, "Please God. Let me win the lottery." Finally, God becomes fed up with the supplicant and speaks through the statue, saying, "If you want to win the lottery, *you have to buy a ticket.*"

My point is, how can any broker expect to sell a home if they're not there to facilitate the process? If the expression that "90 percent of success is showing up" is true, then 90 percent of the brokers failed today. Their extensive knowledge matters not if they weren't here to exercise it. They blew it.

What's ironic is, these same brokers will go to training classes and hire consultants and they'll rack their brains to figure out how they could tweak their marketing or enhance their social media presence or broaden their market acumen, trying to automate a business that works best in face-to-face settings, where most of the battle is won by just be-ing there.

And I know *that* is why I outsell them all. I say it again and again, there's a reason 99 percent of the business is done by 1 percent of the brokers.

Do you want to be in the 1 percent?

Good. You're on the right track.

///

PART SEVEN

Don't Let Little Problems Affect Big Deals

Regardless of how clear the path from A to Z may seem, running into a roadblock is inevitable en route to the deal. The way you handle the little problems will have a direct impact on how you're perceived about managing the larger issues.

Create strategies for navigating around or capitalizing on anything that feels like a problem, because it might just be a solution in disguise. Anything you encounter, whether it's a shift in the market or a challenge to your reputation, can be handled when

you make the decision to not sweat the small stuff.

And sometimes, when you take a step back for bet-

ter perspective, you might just realize that Richard

Carslon, Ph.D., was right, and it's all small stuff.

—— /// ——

FORTY-FOUR

A Little Face Time
Goes a Long Way

I drop off the Commodore and realize I'm so close to one of my favorite clients that I call him and quickly confirm that I'm about to swing by.

My client is a surgeon as well as an attorney, with a half-billion dollars in real estate holdings . . . just your classic underachiever.

I love this guy.

The Surgeon is so used to dealing with life and death in his position at the hospital that he's utterly laid back in every other aspect of his world. (Imagine the Dude from *The Big Lebowski* . . . only if he were on the *Forbes* list.) One of the reasons he's selling his unit is because everyone in the building hates him because he does whatever he wants. The co-op board is always on him about wearing his bathrobe through the lobby when he goes down to the pool. His attitude is, "I can't be worrying about that shit. Life goes on, man."

Anyway, the Surgeon's having some issues with his buyer, so I'm here to smooth things over. One of the reasons he purchases each new property from me is because I cater to him. I could chat with him on the phone, but I'd rather solve his problems in person; it's more expedient. This practice helped establish me as the guy he uses for everything and keeps me there.

My Platt grandparents lived in this building for years, so as I pull up to the place, Ramon, the valet, greets me by name. It's odd to be addressed as "Mr. Flagg" by people who've known me since I was a turtleneck-clad tween. I wave him off, choosing instead to park the car myself. As soon as I pull into the garage, I hear—and feel—a massive scraping sound coming from the roof. Apparently, my G-Wagon is too tall for the garage's clearance. Perhaps that's why Ramon was so adamant about handling this for me.

Well . . . lesson learned.

In my rearview mirror, I see Ramon peering at me from the porte cochere. He's trying to send me a message, likely, "You should have left your car with me, idiot."

This building is the only co-op in the area. Its exclusivity is its selling point, as three residents must provide recommendations for permission to buy here. This building is one of my favorite places to list and show because it is the embodiment of elegance and sophistication.

Anyway, I head up to the Surgeon's unit and I'm greeted by his little rescue dog, a tiny, white, trembly creature with cataracts, a rhinestone collar, and a propensity for ankle biting. She's cute and she never breaks the skin, so it's fine.

The Surgeon welcomes me into his home, which features massive windows, an open concept floor plan, and a rug that really ties the room together. Unfortunately for the buyers, the rug does not convey.

The Surgeon's buyers are currently trying his nerves, and that's a hard thing to do. They're an anxious older couple relocating from New York, and they're taking out all their stress about a cross-country move on my seller, calling him half a dozen times a day with nit-picking requests.

The couple did their final inspection and found some esoteric issues, like a desire to change the HEPA filters. As the deal was already finished, the Surgeon is under no obligation to address these small problems, especially the HEPA problem as that's the building's purview; but he's a good guy and wants to help them. I represent both the buyer and seller (hello, 5 percent!) so I'm anxious to keep everyone happy.

We catch up for a few minutes before I make some calls to work out resolutions and accommodations that please everyone. Again, I could have done this from the car, but it comes across as better service if I do it in person.

Conflicts resolved, I mention how I got stuck going into the garage, and the Surgeon explains I should likely expect this to happen on the way out too. I guess a few paint scratches are the cost of doing business on this level.

As we say our goodbyes, the Surgeon wants to meet with me on Friday so I can show him new properties, but I'm going to Disneyland with my friends, artist Alex Israel, socialite Maria Bell, and Crystal Kung Minkoff, one of the new *Real Housewives of Beverly Hills*.

As this is L.A., he recognizes this a legitimate excuse, and we schedule a time on Saturday instead.

The Surgeon abides.

—— /// ——

FORTY-FIVE

Change Management

The market has changed so much since I started in real estate. The good news is, people have more money, so prices are up. But that also means there's more brokers, and people have access to properties due to technology, so there's more competition. I must be more on top of my game than ever, always innovating. The best brokers are agile and ready to react to change.

In my market, people realize that Beverly Hills is more valuable than they ever thought it was before, even though I suspected we were always underpriced. Still, folks would complain about L.A.'s unreasonable prices in general, even when they were far lower. Back then, I tried to tell buyers, "Anything you buy will be worth ten times more in twenty years, so why are you losing a property because you think you're overpaying for it? The market is in today's dollars—you always have to think about the future."

My advice to buyers now is, if you're always contemplating the future, you must realize that you can never overpay for a property you plan to hold around here. Buy prime, prime, prime real estate because you'll always do well.

Always buy the best location you can afford. Of course, get the best deal you can get, and if you're forced to pay retail, you pay retail, but buy the most you can afford. Be prepared to pay as much as you can with the caveat that you don't put yourself in a position where you can't afford it.

I felt the pinch when the bottom dropped out of the market in 2008, even though I deal with so many high-end people who avoid mortgages by paying cash. While I was fine, I wasn't *fantastic*, and that's a problem. The crash should not have affected my business at all, but it still did. Even the most insulated among us had a slight downtick. I think when people are in a mood not to buy real estate, they just don't buy it, even though there's no reason not to buy. It's almost like a guy that's holding up a sign that says "Buy real estate now. Don't buy real estate now." There's never a reason not to buy. If the market's down, it's a great opportunity. If the market's up, buy because it's going to keep going higher.

Honestly, it's all mental. People can control the markets. If they just wake up one day and say to themselves, "Let's start buying real estate," they could change the market from a down one to an up one. Just look at the boom here during COVID. But during normal times, everyone is scared to be the first. They wait around for the next guy to make the move, and when no one makes that move, that's why the market can be in a down position for time periods.

Still, like in 2008 when the market was down, people stopped seriously looking. Their attitude was, "Oh, it's a down market, let's not buy right now." They'd get nervous that it would keep getting worse; but ultimately, it bounced back. It's all mental—and it always bounces back.

What's good about a down market is, all the trash brokers are weeded out, because the people who can't afford to stay afloat are the ones who aren't real brokers, or they're people who are just relying on family members to toss them a deal here and there. They can't stay in business, and a down market sweeps them away.

(Don't be a trash broker, or a trash anything. Every market has its downtime, make sure you're well positioned to succeed, no matter what the market is doing.)

During that time, even though I had the means to wait out a market recovery, I didn't have the patience. I stepped up my advertising efforts and followed up with anyone who'd every bought or sold a home with me. I found creative ways to be in contact with potential buyers, using strategies like my 1942 project. Even though I hate them, I even threw themed open houses, anything to capture attention. I did whatever I could to keep up the momentum, and when it was quiet, I spent my time studying, understanding that the more I knew, the better I'd be at selling once the market regained its footing. I didn't let the time go to waste.

The key is to be someone who can weather a down cycle. Don't be defeatist. Take your anxiety and turn that negative energy into creating a contingency plan. If you have extra time because business is slow, improve your skills—get certifications or take classes.

When times are good, make accommodations for when they aren't. Instead of taking your commissions all at once and buying yourself something shiny (it's tempting), set up a payroll system and give yourself a weekly salary out of it. Not only does having a set amount coming in take care of payroll taxes, but it also removes the uncertainty of when you'll be paid next.

Structure your business for the long haul so you can weather short-term blips in the market, because the one sure thing about the market is it's ever changing.

FLAGG THIS

Do you work on commission only? If so, how do you manage your commission payouts?

Describe your plan B to not only survive but thrive in a down market. What can you do to differentiate yourself from other salespeople facing the same struggles?

———— /// ————

FORTY-SIX

The Wrong Way
and the Right Way

When necessary, I will fire a client. Regardless of everyone's best intentions, sometimes a partnership just doesn't work. It's okay, it happens. As a professional dealmaker, it's my job to handle a split like a grown-up, a Gwyneth-and-Chris conscious uncoupling, rather than a dramatic junior high breakup on the school bus coming home from a field trip.

Regardless of how crazy or unreasonable a client acts, an amicable parting should be my aim, because word gets around if it isn't.

Handle it the right way and this roadblock disappears in my rearview mirror.

This isn't one of those stories. (Cue the *Law and Order* "dun-dun" sound.)

In the mid-2000s, I worked with a woman from Beverly Hills. She was selling her home, but she wanted to purchase another before she'd accept an offer, and I was to handle both transactions. Double commission? Yes, please.

The problem was, *she* couldn't commit to anything, at least not long term. We saw what felt like hundreds of listings. When we'd find the

One, she'd make an offer and we'd begin the escrow process. This happened six times.

To repeat, we went into escrow *six times*. Six times is four to five times too many.

Mrs. Indecisive found fault with each place over the smallest details once we went into escrow. Mind you, there were no major inspection issues with any of these homes, as we were dealing with luxury properties and reasonable sellers who were happy to make the fixes or give credits. But Mrs. Indecisive was practically demanding the current homeowners raze the property and rebuild for reasons like "feng shui" or "I don't like southern exposure, can we rotate the way the house faces?" Or "Essentially it's a great house, but can you ask the sellers to put a second story on the property in the request for repair?" Umm, yes, this woman likely would have proceeded with this one property on North Camden had the sellers added a second floor for her.

Point is, no, bitch. We can't.

Her reasoning for not buying became increasingly bizarre. In one home, she "smelled mold," despite no evidence of water damage in the initial inspection and nothing uncovered by a second inspection from a mold remediation service. Trust me, those guys can find mold anywhere, up to and including on a loaf of sourdough bread in the pantry. Mold is their raison d'être. They exist to find mold. *There was no mold.*

On the third attempt, she found out that someone passed away here. Friends, let me explain further—this person did not die in a mass murder, and there was no evidence she passed because of toxic mold. A little old lady died peacefully in bed at 104 years old in the 1970s in this home. We should all be so fortunate, right? We only discovered this because her children were telling us of the good luck and fortune and energy the house has. The woman said she did not want to live in a house where anyone died.

Again, I don't mean "died of contagious sickness," I don't mean "ancient burial site." I don't mean "mass murder." Literally, a little old lady went gently into that good night after a happy 104 years on this earth.

If you want to talk about a house of good luck, I can't think of a better one! If I make it to 104 and get to die at home instead of a hospital, I'll take it any day!

As the owner is telling this sweet story to us, I watch this person's facial expression change, and I am thinking to myself, "This homeowner has no idea how mercurial this woman is . . . she needs to close her trap right now."

I was right. That was the end of that one . . . and so on and so on we went.

Because I was so young, it hadn't yet occurred to me to play the psychologist. Surely, she had better things to do than to waste my time with a bunch of bogus offers and odd prejudices, right? However, I wasn't sensitive or seasoned enough to put my ego aside and truly dig to find out her issue, because I cared only about me and not about her. Something was preventing her from loving the properties she picked. It wasn't about the houses, and I should have realized that. Instead of mustering up some compassion for her internal toil, I let myself be affected by her erratic behavior and ever-shifting moods.

I finally snapped.

What I should have done was to sit down with her and say, "I feel like we're no longer working well together as a team. I want what's best for you, so let's refer you to a broker who's a better fit."

There is nothing but upside to this approach. First, by acknowledging the problem, it opens lines of communication. It's possible she'd have come clean about her reticence, and I could have salvaged her business. If not, we'd have taken our respective leaves professionally and with no bad blood. Best part, by providing a referral, I'd still receive a percentage of the sale, had she ever decided on a property.

Yeah . . . that's not what happened.

I went full-metal-jacket angry. Not only did I fire Mrs. Indecisive, but I also sent her a scathing email detailing every one of her deficiencies; I'm talking total scorched earth here. She responded with a bizarre Chinese astrology metaphor about a tiger and ox.

A month later, when she purchased a $7 million home (that I had showed her) from another broker, she sent me an email with a Buddha quote.

Believe me, *that* was more painful than any insult she could have leveled at me. But the joke's on her, because I learned far more from the experience than I might have earned.

At least that's what I tell myself.

Let's face it . . . if I could have only held out for one more fucking escrow, I'd have been $175K richer that year. I hate when that happens.

FLAGG THIS

The Buddha says, "Wear your ego like a loose-fitting garment." But he might have just recommended elastic-waist pants because he was fat.

Now here's the story where I got it right.

When I was a little kid, I used to fantasize about surprising my wife with the home I'd built, presenting it to her with a giant red bow tied around it, like I'd seen in a movie with Steve Martin and Goldie Hawn called *The Housesitter*.

In retrospect, there were a few flaws in this dream, largely because I wasn't going to ever have a wife.

Regardless, I loved the idea of presenting a home wrapped in a bow, even if not in the original circumstance.

Back when Edith was still alive, she told me that Elaine, one of her friends, had passed on. At the time, Edith was ninety-one, an age when all her friends were dying off. Too practical to ever be morbid or maudlin, Edith routed all those references to me.

I'd met Elaine several times and she truly was a saint. I could not say the same for her vituperative daughter, who decided she knew everything about the real estate business without ever really having learned the craft. She refused to accept my assessment of her mother's home's worth and insisted on listing it $1 million over my advice.

Well, we got an offer from one of my buyers . . . for the exact price I'd predicted and suggested. Instead of being pleased, the daughter was furious. She told me, "I won't take this offer unless you cut your commission in half. Further, you'll be fired, and I'll use someone else to broker the deal, plus I won't let any of your clients see the place."

She was a real c-word. That's right—commission cutter. (Wait, what c-word were *you* thinking?)

I wanted to tell her to go fuck herself, but Edith counseled me to take the money and run (as any Jewish grandmother with zero interest in pride over dollars in their account would do), so I didn't tell off the daughter. Plus, I didn't want to disappoint the buyers because I just loved the family, so I grudgingly complied with the spawn of Satan, and I was left with only 1.25% commission on the deal on the seller side.

I made the choice to treat this like a bump in the road and not a volcanic crater from which I could not steer away. Choosing to not sweat the small stuff kept my focus clear.

Even though I'd had a bad experience with the sale, I had the presence of mind to not let this affect my buyers. I wanted to reclaim what should be a positive endeavor, and I decided to do something special for them. When we closed escrow, I arranged to have a huge red bow tied around the house. This took more legwork than you might imagine— you can't just stroll into Michael's and ask for thousands of yards of three-foot-wide ribbon.

The ribbon-wrapped home made the exact impression I'd dreamed of as a kid! But grown-up Josh was a savvier marketer, so I made sure the house was photographed for the local paper. What I lost in commission, I made up for in free advertising.

These days, I'm more likely to thank a client for their business by taking them out to a five-star dinner. That way, I get to enjoy it, too, plus I can write off part of the bill. But if the opportunity presents itself for me to be a showman, you can bet I'm all over it, tuxedo clad, top hat in hand.

Unless you're Elaine's daughter. She can still piss off.

———— /// ————

FORTY-SEVEN

A Group of Two or More Joshes Is Called a Mogul

You want to take your sales to the next level?

Some people will advise you to find a mentor.

Personally, I think you're better off finding yourself a nemesis.

I'm not kidding—having someone in your sights is one of the best things you can do for your own motivation. For instance, if you're running on a treadmill at the gym, aren't you more likely to bump up the intensity if someone you perceive to be older/weaker/slower than you suddenly starts sprinting like a gazelle on the machine next to yours?

Hate has nothing to do with the equation—that adjacent runner might be a lovely person, witty and kind, with a generous streak a mile wide. You don't have to *despise* them; just wanting to *beat* them will quicken your pace.

For me, that catalyst was *MDLLA* cast member Josh Altman. When Josh joined the show, the drama between us was real; it's not something we just exaggerated for the cameras. Our dislike was instant and intense. He thought I was a lackadaisical, spoiled rich kid, and I thought he was boorish and oily. He wore awful ties, paired with horrible maroon suits, and he drove an extremely ostentatious Rolls-Royce and . . . okay, I guess I can stop now. I like the guy, so I don't have to overkill it . . . like he used to overkill his personal aesthetic.

Josh proved to be the perfect nemesis because we were always competing for the same listings. While it didn't feel like it at the time, his presence became a blessing. My desire to crush him made me up my game. I honed my skills because I wanted to beat him. I figured out he couldn't swoop in on my expired listings if I were making doubly sure my clients had their every need met. Happy buyers and sellers can't be poached.

Our feud went on for years, on and off camera. We were professional enough to be polite when we were forced together on a deal, but there was no love lost. And a fight over a stolen client escalated into the Slap Heard 'Round the World a few seasons ago.

Eventually, I began to grudgingly respect his attitude, and he my savoir faire. He realized I wasn't lazy. I came to respect his degree of hustle. The thing about having a nemesis is, the intensity can't remain at the same level. Either it entirely explodes, leading to career-limiting actions (or prison), or it begins to mellow and fade.

After Josh was married and had children, we started to view each other a little differently.

As our lives changed, our priorities shifted.

We stopped taking ourselves so seriously.

We let down our collective guards.

We became friends; we even got our own *MDLLA* spin-off, the aptly named *Josh & Josh*.

While at the core of it, we'll always be each other's nemesis, it's become a running joke rather than a testosterone-charged standoff. We continue to clash, but it's funny now, more like what you'd see from an old married couple than mortal enemies.

Do we still relish every professional opportunity we have to knock each other into the dirt?

Absolutely.

The difference is, if one of us knocks the other down, we'll help the other get back up.

Now, it wasn't just Josh I had an issue with, although ours was my greatest rivalry. I used to eschew friendships with all other brokers. I didn't want anyone to get a leg up on me, so I avoided fraternizing. I assumed other agents would poach my listings and talk shit about me behind my back to clients.

That was a mistaken assumption for two reasons.

First, a satisfied client won't jump ship just because some other broker chats them up. My competency creates their loyalty. Second, having friends in the know is an invaluable resource.

When I became a cast member on *MDLLA*, I started spending time with other brokers. What I found was, I *liked* being around other people in my field. Having a few key friends who understand what I do is a powerful resource. I like being able to call them to share info on pocket listings, on who's in escrow, and on what's happening behind the scenes, and I'm always quick to reciprocate.

All my real estate friends are top brokers, so their wins spur healthy competition within our group. We drive each other to be better at what we do and more informed on how we do it, so the ultimate winners are our clientele. These brokers are exactly who I called to brag about my dinner plans tonight, because it's not just a potential win for me, it's a win for all of us. (Yet as I think about this pending meal, my stomach twists. Is it anxiety? Excitement? Too many Diet Cokes? Too soon to tell.)

Now, I am not saying you should pal around with all your peers. Some of them suck. Those people aren't to be invited into my inner circle and that's okay. There's value in having a nemesis. I dislike plenty of my peers, and there's always at least one person that I despise and want to grind into a fine paste.

Sometimes whom I hate is just as important as whom I like. But when I made the decision to minimize the aggravation and maximize the enjoyment, my worst nemesis became a great friend.

Of course, no deal is considered closed until the contract is inked, regardless of how chummy you are with all involved. Handshakes are worthless . . . unless you're looking for an expedient way to spread germs.

I made the mistake of not getting everything in writing when I was still a rookie. I made assumptions that would eventually bite me in the ass. For example, I'd think, "Oh, we're friends, they will totally give me the listing," or "I've known them forever, I'll take them at their word."

Wrong.

In high-stakes sales, I can't be sure of anything not legally enforceable. I learned that when dealing with numbers this high, people will do whatever is most beneficial to their pocketbook, regardless of handshakes, friendships, history together, and so on.

I can't stress this enough: friends respect each other enough to put it in writing.

—————— /// ——————

FORTY-EIGHT

Professor Edith's School of Hard Knocks

Edith was a master class in not sweating the small stuff, and no one was better at negotiating than she was. I suppose this is because when she was a young woman, she was most often bargaining for her life. She must have grown accustomed to dealing with impossible stakes—and what other choice did she have but to try to press on?

During the war, she hid in plain sight with false papers, working as a Red Cross nurse. In reality, the woman's name she was using was a lady who died in a concentration camp. She needed someone's identity card, so she stole it.

Edith was permitted to travel through the Netherlands when wearing her nurse uniform, so she never took it off. Once, she and an older neighbor were out on their bikes trying to find food when they passed a tent marked *Kommandantur*. Instead of seeing this as a roadblock, Edith considered this an opportunity to get something she desperately needed, so she told the friend, "Play along with me. Whatever I do, go with it," as she strode right into a tent full of Nazi officers. Her friend was panicked, but Edith left her no choice but to comply.

After announcing herself with a heel click and a *Heil, Hitler*, Edith pretended to be a tad bit insane, twitching and jerking, crying about coming from Hamburg where her home had just been bombed. She spoke to the officer in perfect German, because Edith understood the importance of mirroring the actions of the person she was negotiating with. It was imperative she make him believe they were of the same tribe.

Edith, if you have not gathered, was ballsy. This woman used to swim in the lake in the morning pretending to be a German Red Cross nurse, and she would eavesdrop on the Nazis. The Nazis had no idea they were splashing around with a little Jewish girl. This was also a woman who dug a tunnel into a concentration camp through the latrines in order to get people out, including my grandfather. Sadly, he could not escape, and that's why my real grandfather died in Auschwitz. People don't know my dad's real father's name is Stein. Hans Stein, my grandfather and my dad's dad, died in the camps, and my grandmother remarried Eric Flegenheimeer (Flagg), who had been in the Dutch Resistance with her.

Edith always swung for the fences—a trait that would carry on her entire life. She said to the officer, "It's Christmas and I want to bring food to my family. Do you think you could write me a note for my mother and me so we can get back to Amsterdam without any problems? We don't want to be stopped and questioned."

And ostensibly, slaughtered.

Not only did she have the audacity to request a note, but she also told that officer what to write, explaining that it should say she and her mother (read: friend) could have free passage throughout the country. Her resolve was such that it didn't occur to the officer to question her. Then she distracted him with effusive gratitude before he could put a date on the note.

See, Edith didn't just want free passage that day—she wanted it in perpetuity. She knew how valuable that piece of paper would be for her work with the underground. The officer was so touched by her plight (read: performance) that he kissed her cape before he left them. Edith eventually even used the note to catch train rides with the Nazis instead of having to pedal her bike everywhere. The Nazis literally helped her impede their progress, and they had no clue, all because she had the temerity to ask. They made the crucial error of underestimating her.

FLAGG THIS

In what ways has your fear held you back professionally?

What's the worst thing that could happen if you didn't ask for what you needed?

Compare this result to the best-case scenario, in which you get everything you want—is the risk worth the reward?

How might others underestimate you, and how can you use this to your advantage?

What circumstances in your life can help you steel your own resolve?

In Edith's purview, everything was negotiable, understandable given her history. For instance, most people walk into a store, and they pay the price on the tag. You shop retail, you pay retail prices, that's how it works. Neiman Marcus is not a souk . . . unless you're Edith.

Sometimes this attitude would embarrass my parents or me, but mostly I loved watching it. When I was a kid, I couldn't believe what she'd get away with. She'd tell me, "If I gave them shit, they either took it or they didn't take it. Most of the time, they took it."

Once she was in an upscale rug store at the Pacific Design Center. She found one she liked and asked how much it was. The salesman told her the price was $37,500 and Edith replied, "I'll give you $17,000."

The salesman demurred, "No, I can't do that. I'd have to sell a lot of carpets to make up for what I lost if I gave you that price."

She then asked, "How many have you sold today?"

He replied, "None."

She pulled a wad of cash out of her bra and slapped it on the counter. She said, "Now you've sold one."

Another time, Edith was at an auto show. Her accountant had talked her into upgrading her car, so she went to look at Rolls-Royces. It was a big year, she needed write-offs, and they had already given a tremendous amount to charity. She was wearing an outfit she'd sewn herself and a pair of custom sneakers made to accommodate a foot problem. No one would ever guess she once designed the clothes loved by so many stylish American women.

Anyway, Edith saw a model she liked, so she told the British salesman she wanted the car. The salesman kind of blew her off thinking she was full of shit. "Madam, I can't sell you this car, it's our floor model. We need it here."

She called our business manager, Steve Sobul, and asked him to come to the Beverly Hills Hotel where they were doing a showing of all the latest Rolls-Royce models and meet her with a cashier's check. Such was her shrewdness, she had the check made out for less than what they were asking for the car. She came back and said, "Here's a check for the car, and make sure it's gassed up and ready for me to drive home by 5:00 p.m."

FYI, Edith would have paid for the car in cash, but her bra wasn't big enough. She kept everything in there, including Kleenex. If I ever had a sniffle, she'd hand me one and say, "Don't worry, it's clean." It wasn't. Her tissues were always filled with lipstick and moist from her constantly rubbing her nose.

Edith was the ultimate eccentric, and she presented herself that way on purpose; the war taught her the power of being underestimated. While she had beautiful things, she couldn't be bothered to wear them. She didn't need to look the part; she wasn't vain. Instead, she knew her worth as a person and was never afraid to inform others of it. She did so much for the Jewish community in Los Angeles that there was no question she was a fantastic human being. Not only did this woman give millions to charity, but she gave time, and that is equally as important. Now I'm not saying she was sitting there all day long slaving away volunteering; she was running a business, but she did what she could until she retired. And, until shortly before she died, she volunteered in the emergency room at Cedars!

Edith wasn't one of those people who lived through the Holocaust and then never talked about it afterward. Oh, you could not shut her up about it. She'd tell you about it within the first four minutes, if not four seconds, of meeting you. One time she was in Paris and her cab driver started to grumble about Americans. Edith wasn't having it. She told him to stop the cab (which was super uncomfortable as it wasn't even a cab; it was a driver from the Ritz and we had to use him for the rest of our trip). She said, "The Americans, who saved your ass after the war; go fuck yourself." Then she got out of the car and walked the rest of the way.

Edith was never upset when people made the wrong assumptions about her; instead, she was amused. Another time, she was in the elevator in her building, leaving her Century City penthouse while carrying her dry cleaning. Some pompous man tried to stop her, saying that cleaning staff had to use the service elevator. Edith refused to get off and didn't believe the neighbor was entitled to an explanation. She simply stood her ground and continued to ride as he worked himself into a lather. She just smiled and nodded. She was far too elegant to talk to the guy (which is ironic coming from a woman who would bite your head off in one second). They stepped outside at the same time and her doorman rushed up, saying, "I've pulled your Rolls around, Mrs. Flagg." She tossed her laundry basket in the backseat and then winked at her assumptive neighbor. The man was mortified. Instead of being offended, Edith was delighted every time she was able to hide in plain sight.

At the height of her business, Edith owned one of the few garment companies with benefits, like full health insurance and profit sharing. She believed in taking care of her workers. So she was hurt and offended when the union came in and tried to organize her factory.

Mostly, she was angry.

After planning an attack with a labor lawyer, she instructed her secretary to hire the "dirtiest, smelliest, roughest, and toughest guys you can find" to serve as her bodyguards to protect her from the strikers. She set up fake delivery trucks, and workers wheeled around empty clothing racks covered in black tarps, meant to foil strikers when they tried to throw paint on the merchandise.

I was young then, but I remember being fascinated by her new collection of wigs, toupees, and mustaches. Edith wasn't about to be scared away from her office. My grandmother was such a boss she would go down the elevator from the executive offices at the Cooper Building and onto Los Angeles Street in downtown and stand in front of the picketers. She'd spit seeds from her grapes on the ground right in front of the picketers' feet in order to piss them off, hoping one of them would be enraged enough to hit her, because once they did that, she'd win and they'd lose and the union could not take control. All she needed was for one of them to touch her and the picket was over. Her motto was, "I beat Hitler, and I will beat these motherfuckers, too." She had the balls to drive downtown in the middle of a strike in her Rolls as the strikers threw things at her car. That was her way of telling them to fuck off. What made her so angry was how progressive she was. Long before other companies adopted the practice, my grandmother had profit-sharing plans, full health benefits, and treated these people with the utmost respect.

During the strike, she would don a wig and mustache, and she, my uncle Ilan, my father, and a few of the executives would roll racks of garments out of the factory in trucks, and she would drive the truck. No one knew Mrs. Flagg was behind the wheel in a wig and mustache.

When the employees who'd picketed asked for their jobs back, Edith was steadfast. She'd already replaced them. She wouldn't even consider giving them another chance—she couldn't forgive those who had the best salaries and benefits accusing her of being unfair to them. She left no room for negotiation.

Ultimately, the courage of Edith's convictions and view of her own worth came from how she'd survived and what she created. She wasn't confident because she had the nerve to ask, the *asking* is what gave her the confidence. I've said it before, actions don't follow motivation; motivation follows action.

So much of my mindset comes from growing up between my parents and Edith. I'm who I am because of her. She taught me to never accept a first offer, even if it was great, and the importance of asking for more. I have so much respect for what she endured and accomplished. What sticks with me most is her resolve. If she ever ceded her ground, she'd have never survived the business world, let alone the Holocaust.

What I'm saying is, if Edith could be Edith with all she had to endure, I can certainly power past what's annoying or uncomfortable, and so can you.

—————— /// ——————

FORTY-NINE

Rubber Chicken

Charitable giving is my go-to strategy for not sweating the small stuff. When I know that I'm supporting something greater than myself, it puts all the minutia into proportion.

Giving back is incredibly important to me. I grew up watching my parents and grandparents donate generous amounts of time and money, so my family has ingrained the notion of charity in me since birth. Believe me, I spent a lot of my childhood wearing turtlenecks to boring award dinners. That's because charitable giving is a tenet of Judaism, not only in our religion but also our culture. Giving back is what we do. Eating bad chicken dinners in ballrooms en masse is a byproduct of that.

Within Judaism, we Jews are required to take care of struggling family members before we extend ourselves to external sources. Truly, charity begins at home. Once the deadbeats in our clans are set, we turn our generosity outward. I am obligated to give to my community, both through Jewish law and upbringing. It's not a choice.

The Talmud dictates that Jews tithe at least 10 percent to charity, although the rule is to not give more than one fifth of one's income to avoid the danger of becoming destitute oneself. Perhaps not so coincidentally, this is also a prerequisite to get into any Jewish country club worth belonging to in Los Angeles, so this is another why reason people do it.

Charity is considered a mitzvah—a good deed—and tzedakah is the concept that philanthropy is as much a benefit to the donors as the recipients. That literally means the reason for giving does not matter. The act itself is what counts because we believe *mitzvah goreret mitzvah*—one good act will spur another.

It's my understanding that WASPier religions prefer to write their checks quietly, anonymously. Not my people. Flaunt that shit, baby! If the charity gives you the opportunity to put your name on a building you better make sure it's a neon sign with shining bulbs! For example, if a Jew decides to donate an entire hospital wing specifically to see his or her name on the building? That is a mitzvah. Our reasons why—no matter how self-serving—are eclipsed by the good a hospital wing will do.

Charitable giving is kind of like the ultimate get-out-of-jail-free card.

If we choose to give so much that we're honored at an event with rubbery poultry? Also a mitzvah.

If we write a massive check for no reason other than having our names published at the top of the donor list *specifically* to rub our success in our rivals' faces? Welcome to Mitzvah City, Population: Us.

Two things to note here: first, while I disagree, I can see how this philosophy made the Jews less than popular in the world's estimation over the centuries, and second, this is a loophole I definitely exploit.

For instance, let's say you have a thousand rich Jews in Beverly Hills, and you invite them all to a big charity event. The main sponsor gets his or her name at the top of the banner on the dais. I like to make sure that person is me. If I find out the billionaires are donating $5,000 to $10,000, then I'll do $25,000 because there's a lot of exposure there. I want *my* name on the banner in addition to wanting that $25,000 to help others. (Had to throw that one in there to make myself look human, you know?)

In the Jewish culture, giving is not an either/or proposition.

I look at it like this—do I want to spend $25,000 on publicity where that cash does nothing but benefit the publicist's employer, or do I want to take that $25,000 to shelter, clothe, and feed elderly Jews while simultaneously benefiting from the good PR coming from having my name attached? It's a no-brainer.

Given Edith's experience, the bulk of my giving goes to Jewish causes, and especially for Holocaust education. The ADL (Anti-Defamation League) tracks incidences of bias and aggression toward Jews, and they report huge spikes in anti-Semitism. Hate crimes against Jews have been surging in the aftermath of violence between Hamas and Israel. This is a major concern to Jews all around the world. The best tool against this rising tide is education, and that takes funding.

When I got on the board of the Holocaust Museum L.A., I suggested I be the honoree that year, and they agreed because they saw me as someone who could bring more attention to the cause. Yes, that's right folks, I suggested they honor myself . . . because that's super normal. So, I wrote a check, and then I got to speak at a dinner. (How was the chicken there? Chewy.) Also, I may be self-deprecating, but please know that any charity I am involved in gets the full benefit of my time, energy, and attention. I don't just cut a check.

What's important was that the donation was earmarked to help lessen instances of hate through programming, which is a growing concern in our current social climate where anti-Semitic incidents have spiked alarmingly. Of course, the additional benefit was speaking in front of hundreds of qualified buyers. I do overplay this a bit, but I have to say I truly am involved with these charities; I do more than just write checks. This is a part of my shtick, but you get the point. I'm probably more involved than anyone I know my age because it is important to me. (But, full disclosure, I still do like that name on the plaque.)

Of course, I took it one step further and placed an ad on the cover of the *L.A. Times*'s real estate section to tout my honor. You know why? Because I can't let a single instance to sell myself pass.

Personally, I can't place an ad congratulating myself; it's untoward. It's not chic. What I've previously done was to pay for an ad that said, "Rodeo Realty congratulates Josh Flagg on his blah, blah, blah." You know how *Variety* magazine congratulates all these celebrities? Imagine if the celebrity just paid for the ad, taking it out, and writing that *Variety* is congratulating them. Same thing.

Whatever you choose to give, embrace the notion of mitzvahs begetting mitzvahs and be sure to get your name on the donation. You're allowed to have your charitable gift do more than just make you feel good, at least according to my people. And the more good you do, the less you'll be bothered by some of the day-to-day nonsense. You'll be powered by a higher purpose.

If you're not liquid enough yet to give a recognized amount, save up and make a larger donation later. For example, you could be a $1,000-level donor to your college once a year for five years, or you could be a $5,000-level donor once. You'll stand out with the bigger donation, attracting more attention from classmates with whom you want to do business. (Or that sorority girl who turned down your invitation to the barn dance.) What matters is you're doing good work—why not let your generosity reflect positively back on you? If you're one of those people who goes around quoting Ayn Rand—believe me, I am not—you might ascribe to her theory that altruism couldn't be the standard for moral behavior, which she believed was "incompatible with freedom, with capitalism, and with individual rights."

Listen, don't be the buzzkill that goes around spouting off about Objectivism. Make the donation, take the tax break, and let them put your name on the program; it's just a no-brainer.

The anticipation of a mitzvah from giving reinforces the million-dollar mindset. I work harder to close every deal because I'm not just fighting so I can buy another Billy Haines piece. Instead, I'm negotiating to aid Jews everywhere. If you went into every negotiation knowing that what you'd earn on the deal could not only pay for your boat but also help to feed the hungry, save shelter dogs, or cure childhood cancer, wouldn't you give it your all? Wouldn't you be relentless? Wouldn't you do everything in your power to come to an agreement?

The mindset is a game changer, so go ahead and change the game—everyone benefits, including you. When you realize you're working for more than just yourself, it's easy to put those nagging little things into perspective.

As I pull back into my driveway after meeting with the Surgeon, I notice the bees have returned, this time with reinforcements. But I choose not to view them as a problem. Instead, I decide to appreciate their role in pollinating my flowers.

PART EIGHT

///

Play the Psychologist

Understanding human behavior is the strategy that keeps on giving. Whether skilled negotiators realize it or not, they're psychologists at heart, able to identify and manipulate a deal by influencing buyers.

While no one likes to be coerced, smart dealmakers subtly encourage the other party to think they're in control.

The best dealmakers put themselves in their buyers' shoes, attempting to understand and empathize with what drives them.

But sometimes we dealmakers need to take a step back and analyze our own behaviors too.

—— /// ——

FIFTY

Power Struggle

Before I head out again, I need to take a conference call with a couple other big brokers about a colisting. In terms of sales, the three of us are at approximately the same level, so there tends to be a lot of posturing within the group. The few times we've gotten together have been like the scene from *American Psycho* where all the stockbrokers compare the embossing and font on each other's business cards. It's ridiculous, in the best possible way, and yet I still need my metaphorical cardstock to be the thickest.

Claire and I are working in the dining room because I can spread out from one end of the table to the other. I have her dial me into the phone bridge, and I offer a greeting once connected.

"Josh here."

No one answers. My voice echoes in the emptiness.

Shit. I'm first. I can't be the first person on the call. I hang up.

"Claire, can you patch me in again in two minutes?"

I stare down at the minute hand on my Patek and wait for the appropriate amount of time to pass.

I realize this sounds insane. I do. And how hard would it have been for me to read my emails while I sat on the phone bridge? I can't preach about the merits of efficiency and then deliberately waste my own time, right?

Wrong.

What you might not understand is, so much of the real estate business, really, so much about dealmaking, is theater. This is a power play, pure and simple. And me making them wait for me to arrive now will translate into my having the upper hand for my clients when we're ready to negotiate the sale.

Two minutes could mean hundreds of thousands of dollars later.

When I get on the call one hundred and twenty seconds later, everyone's waiting for me. Exactly like it should be.

Patrick Bateman/Josh Flagg/my clients: 1.

Everyone else: 0.

///

FIFTY-ONE

Be the Jedi

The more I worked with clients, the more I saw patterns emerge. I began to learn that the questions they'd answer would tell only half of the real story. Watching their nonverbal clues and listening to what they *didn't* say would prove as, if not more, illuminating than what they said.

Early on, I learned that some clients are pleasers, feigning enthusiasm about anything I'd show them. In the beginning, I'd interpret their affable nature as interest, to my detriment. I'd think I sold a listing, only to have them come up with half-hearted excuses as to why they couldn't buy it. They never wanted the house, but I wrongly conflated their need to please with an urge to buy.

That's when I started baiting my listing appointments with bad first houses. I needed these clients to understand that the only way I could help them was if they told me how they really felt and not what they thought I wanted to hear. By showing them I hated a listing, I gave them permission to be more negative, as getting their true thoughts helped me find them the right place.

To be a successful dealmaker, you must become a Jedi.

Rather, become a Jedi you must.

Once I ask the right questions and pay attention to the answers, I'll know the best way to proceed. For buyers, this means I'll determine a small set of homes that will be the perfect fit for their lifestyle and bud-get. For sellers, I'll have a roadmap to the exact course of action we need to follow for a quick sale. But sometimes the process is so overwhelming for both kinds of clients, they just shut down and lose all decision-making abilities. The very worst call here is to hard sell—attempt to coerce a client to expedite the process, and they will disappear into the ether; I promise you this.

So the way to get clients to come around to my way of thinking is to make them believe whatever I suggest was their idea in the first place. To be clear, all my professional actions are for my clients' benefit, so I never want anything that's counter to their best interests. Yet for what-ever reason, people don't always choose to listen to the expert, so I must work around their flawed decision by playing the long game.

Here's what I tell people who are getting ready to sell their home. Price it right, stage it if you have ugly shit, and don't get emotional. Price it to excel with multiple offers, or price with a little meat on the bone, but don't ask too much because you're just going to end up reducing it. Sometimes I suggest fixing the landscaping or repainting. The best sell-ers are amenable when I talk to them, largely because I buffer the sug-gestions with compliments. I'll say, "You and I, we're simpatico. We have excellent taste. But because of the buyer pool, we need to make your slate as blank as possible, so it appeals to all people. Not everyone has our superior level of taste."

I might think to myself, "I would never put your hideous gold leaf Beaux-Arts Victorian chair in my home," but they don't need to know that.

In a perfect world, my sellers would leave the house and take their terrible furniture with them so I could have the place staged. Unfortu-nately, that's not always an option, so I must work around it when I show their home to potential buyers. I'll respect their position, but then a month later, if we haven't made progress specifically because they didn't heed my advice and remove their hideous furnishings, I'll say, "You know what? I was thinking about what you told me in that meet-ing. You are so smart. Even though I love your taste, you were right. I really think you should box up your personal items and make the space more neutral."

Then they do just that because they thought they came up with the idea themselves.

Easy peasy.

PART NINE

—— /// ——

Never Take
the First Offer

Jumping at the first offer is a sign of weakness. The best deals are made when you have buyers at the edge of their seats, hoping the deals come to them. You won't always have multiple offers, but you can almost always eke out a little extra if you put in the time and effort. You're in the hot seat up until the point when you have an offer on the table. When you've got even one interested party, the power shifts to you because the buyer doesn't know the cards you're holding, and you can use that to your advantage.

It all goes back to confidence, stemming from the trust your clients place in you.

Fighting for your client isn't just a part of your responsibility but a negotiator's best asset. Your interested buyer is sweating now, so play that up to your advantage. But take some time and remind yourself that there's always another deal around the corner.

—————— /// ——————

Another Satisfied Customer

"Shelby, what do you like most about me?"

"Hi, Josh! Um . . . I guess I like how you never waste time with hellos and you just launch into whatever you need to say," Shelby says, laughing.

Claire and I are back in the car, on the way drop her off at the office before I go home to prep for my client dinner. Shelby, a current and favorite buyer, is on speakerphone. After I explain to her that I'm writing a book and I secure permission to quote her as long as I change her name (which I do), I ask her perspective on our working relationship.

Shelby, her husband, and their small children are relocating from out east. Mr. Shelby is about to become fully vested in the tech company he helped found. The Shelby family is currently rich, but they're two months away from becoming wealthy. Their debate is, do we buy a home like we're rich or like we're wealthy?

At their current $10 million budget, they've leaned into the conservative choice of rich. This is a bad call—that's not an opinion, it's fact. They'll be able to afford far more house in fewer than sixty days. The rule in Los Angeles real estate is that you can't go wrong buying as much home as your budget will comfortably accommodate.

I've spent a lot of time with the family, so I'm convinced they will be happier if they up their budget to get more of what they want. Mr.

Shelby expressed a desire to go cheaper and get a "right now" house, where Shelby is thinking longer term and she'd like to start their next chapter in a "forever" home. The best way to accommodate Shelby's wish is to increase their budget. But they must come to this conclusion for themselves; I can't make the decision for them.

I would like to, of course. If everyone listened to me, Crocs would not exist.

Anyway, I've moved along the process by showing them a mixed bag of rich and wealthy houses.

Shelby tells me, "Well, Josh, you know we interviewed a lot of agents. Honestly, we were hesitant to go with a TV star because we're private. We don't want people to know our business."

"Did you hear that, Claire? Shelby says I'm a *star*," I say.

Claire grimaces at me as she takes notes on the call.

"Hey, Claire!" Shelby says. "Anyway, I liked how you called us right away after our initial meeting. You acted like you really wanted our business. I appreciated your work ethic and enthusiasm. The other realtors we talked to, they just sent listings. But you sat us down and wanted to know about us before we started looking at homes. You literally said, 'Tell me everything about you.' You even had us text photos of the other places we've lived. We've moved a lot because of my husband's work, and no one's ever asked us that before."

The most expedient route to determining a buyer's taste is to see what they've previously bought. From their photos, I deduced that Shelby's aesthetic is preppy. The family would be happiest in an old-money, beachy, East Coast, casual-chic home, with a rolling lawn and lots of privacy. They're more likely to find exactly what they want if they increase their budget. The most expedient way to prove this to them was to show them a few places at the low end of their budget, which is why I took them to Shaq's old home, which they loathed. Apparently they were not in the market for a door with a Superman-style S on the knob.

The assumption is that I just want to sell *something*. While that is true, I aim to sell the *perfect* something. Having buyers seeing imperfect first is a foil to how good the homes that come next will be.

Again, it's a ballet and you can call me Baryshnikov. Nine out of ten times, the person I sell the house to is coming back to me when they resell the house in five or ten years. If I sell them shit, it's going to be super uncomfortable when I can't get them out of the house those years later. So, keep that in mind, folks. What seems easy now to sell them might be a bitch in a few years, and they may not be so keen to work with you when you can't resell it for them without taking a loss. (And yes, I realize it is tempting when you see that commission check waving in your face.)

FLAGG THIS

What simple but relevant actions can you take to prove your trust-worthiness to your clients?

"I also appreciate how you're always sending us listings so we can drive past first. You know how important neighborhood is because of our kids, and you're so conscious about our time. We don't care how great a house is on the inside if it's not well located."

Exactly. Hers is not the only time I'm saving.

"What else? Okay, you've educated us on how the house itself is a depreciating value. The finishes don't ever get newer; they get more used. And contemporary homes get 'tired.' You make us consider what the dirt is worth. Now, every time we see a place, my husband and I ask each other, 'How much is the dirt worth?' In the beginning, we'd ask you, 'What do you think the dirt is worth?' but you explained that's a question we needed to decide as a family. You said you could give us a number, but it would be irrelevant because then we'd think that was the price you were telling us we should pay, putting the onus on you. But, you also stress that we should make offers. In this process, you've taught us that 'shooters gotta shoot' and that we'll miss 100 percent of the shots we don't take. So . . . that brings us to Camden."

The home on Camden is a $14.5 million property, and it's exactly the home they should purchase; it ticks all the boxes.

"We're taking our shot?" I ask. Enough about the book, I have a deal to close.

Shelby is ecstatic. "Yes! How much do we offer?"

We've spoken extensively about offer strategy, and part of that is determining what kind of offer wouldn't offend the seller. Come in too low and they're not even going to counter, putting the whole deal in danger.

To get the lowest price on a home, I go backward, factoring in terms. The best terms will equal the best deal and the best chance a seller will accept. The cleaner the deal, meaning an all-cash offer and waived inspection, equals a lower price and a shorter escrow. When you need the opposite, you're going to pay for that.

In Shelby's case, they sought a more conservative preapproval of $10 million (because they're rich) but in two months, they could spend more like $20 million (because, wealthy). They're also in the process of selling their home in Nantucket. It's about to close, but it's not yet a done deal, so for the moment, they'd need a mortgage contingency.

The Camden home is listed at $16.5 million. I never get too hung up on other brokers' prices because so often they price at what the seller hopes to get rather than what the market will bear. I think I can get Camden somewhere in the mid-$13s. I don't share info this yet, as I don't want to disappoint her. And I'll have to feel out the other broker first.

I tell her, "Give me your best terms for a close in two months. Because of the mortgage contingency and long close, we must sweeten the deal for the seller. That could be a waived inspection or nonrefundable deposit."

"How about we offer a 3 percent deposit now and another 3 percent in thirty days?" she asks.

I reply, "No, let's not tie up your cash. We'll offer 6 percent down, released in thirty days. Let them come back to us and ask us to release a portion now." While this is the same exact amount of a deposit, the Shelbys will come across as more serious buyers if they don't ask to break up that payment. We may well end up going half now and half then, but we'll have more leverage if the sellers are the ones to ask.

Next, a trick that I use with all my buyers to reinforce how committed they are to the property: before we determine an offer price, I make Shelby sell the house to me. That's right, I have *them* pitch *me* on why this is the home they should buy, as though they need my approval. Baller move, yes?

I mention potential downsides of buying this home, pointing out minor flaws, like how the lawn needs to be reseeded. Shelby handily counters my objections. She tells me all the things she loves about it and why she can picture raising her children in what she calls her forever home. She gets emotional, envisioning her life there, patchy grass and all.

Yes. This is it. The *one.*

We finish up by determining the most Shelby and Mr. Shelby are willing to pay is $13.8 million, the sweet spot between what Shelby and Mr. Shelby hope to spend. We say our goodbyes and then I go to work. I call the other broker. He answers on the first ring. I appreciate this.

A quick word about being available by phone?

Always pick up.

My response to a ringing phone is practically Pavlovian. I like to say, "It could be money calling." When people are making one of the biggest decisions of their lives, they don't want to have to wait long to make it. Obviously, there are times to not answer, like in the middle of a listing appointment, but you can bet I'm all over those messages the second I step out the seller's front door.

I tell the seller's broker that I have an offer, but my buyer is stuck in the $12.5s. I say this to feel him out. I want to gauge his reaction. To be clear, this is not a lie; it's a negotiation and it's my obligation as a responsible agent to get the best deal for my buyer. I would be doing them a disservice if I came in any higher at first.

Now, if the notion of starting a negotiation low, instead of coming in at their absolute best offer of $13.8 million makes you uncomfortable, you are not—and will never be—a million-dollar dealmaker. You can't develop the million-dollar dealmaker mindset. Go raise alpacas instead. (Not llamas—they're too mean for you.)

This is how the sausage is made. You're either a carnivore or you aren't.

That the broker doesn't immediately tell me to piss off is a good sign. He balks, but he's not outraged or offended. There's bluster but not fury. Excellent.

As we chat, I do not relay my clients' enthusiasm for this home. Instead, I tell the broker it's a horrible house and it's falling apart and the whole lawn needs to be reseeded. I explain how the clients cannot pay more because they don't want to have to work themselves to death to afford the place.

Again, not a lie; instead, a dance. The other broker is doing his best . . . can you say Nureyev? He tells me that he hears I'm writing a book and it must be fiction if I'm coming to him in the mid-$12s.

Pas de bourrée.

Then he explains how the house has had *a lot* of action lately. Because our negotiation is friendly and professional, I do not reply, "So has your mother." It's just how the ballet is performed.

Pirouette.

The broker then tells me the seller will go with whomever gives them the best deal. (And so will his mom.)

I wait for what I am sure is coming next. If he gives me a caveat, a small opening, I'll know the bluster isn't genuine and that he wants to make a deal as much as I do. (Again, a lot like his mother.)

Wait for it . . . wait for it . . .

The broker says, "Thing is, Josh, the sellers' kids are in school, so they're hoping for a longer escrow."

Rond de jambe.

Like that, the delicate balance of power tips to me. A longer escrow is exactly what Shelby's family needs. But instead of my having to ask for it, he's already offered it. While the sellers may be seeing a lot of interest in their home, it's likely the other interested parties don't want to wait for little Destinee and Horatio to finish the school year.

The broker then tells me the comps justify *at least* $13 million for the home, which is exactly why sellers need a broker who will get them listed at the right price from the beginning. But coming on the market at a higher price could have been their strategy to accommodate for their children finishing school. Not a good one, but still.

I play up my buyers' frugality, saying how they have no emotional attachment to this house. I do not mention Shelby's fantasy about the whole family posing in matching Christmas jammies in front of the home's magnificent hearth.

I'm fishing for a number, and so is he. It's a standoff. Time to apply subtle pressure.

I say to him, "Let's be upfront. This will help how I structure the deal. Just tell me what you know."

"How serious are they?"

"Serious. But they're businesspeople, and they're deciding between a few properties. They will choose the best deal. Period."

An actual lie. They want this house and this house only.

Then the other broker puts the nail in his own coffin, telling me, "No one's trying to get full price. The buyers are just trying to get an offer that's compelling."

Bingo.

That's when I switch from adversarial to convivial. My task has changed. Now I must assure the other broker that he and I? We're on the same team. We want to get this deal done. Together.

I say, "Well . . . the husband wants to write in the mid-$12s, but she's willing to go as high as $13 million. But with a longer escrow, we'd need to land in the $12s."

As a reminder, the buyer is willing to spend up to $13.8 million.

He asks me, "Do you think we can get it done at $13 million?"

"I prepped them for $13 million, but let's be bold."

He sighs because he knows I've got him. He finally replies, "Why don't you write the offer at $12.75 million, and that will give us some room? They're not going to be happy, but . . ."

"Sounds good. We'll get that written up."

We have a deal. While there are plenty of events that could knock us off the rails between now and closing, this is an outstanding first step.

We say our goodbyes and I hang up. I turn to Claire and say, "Shooters gotta shoot."

To which she replies, "Next."

///

FIFTY-THREE

Be Cool, Don't Be All, Like, Uncool

One of the ways I steel myself for a negotiation is to be armed with the most information before doing battle. My goal is always to cede as little as possible, because I'm always trying to get the best deals for my clients, whether they're buying or selling, so I have tactics.

For example, houses aren't usually inspected until after an offer is made, and a bad inspection—or a not-bad inspection and a flighty buyer—can kill a deal. I aim to avoid this with my sellers. Getting ahead of unwelcome news is key here. I often insist my sellers have an inspection before listing. That way, if there's a major issue, we'll know about it, and we can accommodate for it. This knowledge gives the seller—and me—the upper hand. (This tactic is far more effective than crossing your fingers and hoping no one notices the problems, FYI.)

Think about it, what's the purpose of an inspection? To inspect the house? *Wrong.* The *real* purpose of an inspection is it gives the buyer the opportunity to renegotiate with the seller in the middle of escrow. And the seller who is mentally now moved out of their home at that point just wants the deal done so gives in and reduces the price of the property because they just want to close the deal. It's a bait and switch, but the reality is this: if I do the report ahead of time and show it to the buyer, they have no leverage to ask for a price reduction even if they decide to do their own inspections. Because how can they say we want $100K off to replace the roof when we told them ahead of time that the house has a jacked-up roof? One can't argue they need a price reduction when they knew about something before.

This is how you stay one step ahead of the other guy.

Now the buyer can still do their own inspection. In fact, they probably should so that they can't come back later and say we forced them to buy the house without an inspection. But their inspector is not going to come up with anything different than the first inspector that we just hired, so there will be no surprises. Yet we've neatly taken away the buyers' power to ask for a price adjustment, reduction credit, or whatever. As a seller, this is the best fifteen hundred bucks you will ever spend on those reports; and I implore them to do everything: chimney, sewer line, geo, general inspection, and so on. Maybe even bring in a vet to check out the backyard squirrels' health. Get everything in there so the buyer can't come in and try and fuck you in the ninth hour.

Let's say the HVAC system needs to be updated, we can offer a $5,000 credit right upfront. When issues are acknowledged, volunteered, and there's a plan in place to address them, the buyer's broker loses that power to negotiate. They're far less likely to come back demanding a $50,000 credit if we're upfront about the cost from the start. A last-minute concession always costs more.

The best part is, if the other broker demands more credit back when my seller and I have been so upfront, that broker looks unreasonable. Plus, it's a great opportunity for me to pounce. I'll swoop in and make that broker feel like the greedy idiot he or she is.

When a buyer wants the house and the seller wants to sell it, it's infrequent that either party walks away over a few dollars. In the extraordinarily rare instance this happens, like if my seller's offering a $5,000 credit and the buyer is insisting on a $25,000 credit or the deal is off, I'll calmly and dispassionately work with the other broker to split the $20,000 difference if it means we both still walk away with six figures of commission each.

But to be clear, only when death is the other option will I let go of any of my money.

When I'm representing a buyer and their broker won't work with me to find a middle ground on a small gap and I'm confident no one's walking away, I'll take the offensive.

Think about it—a buyer can purchase any home, whereas a seller has only the one property. It behooves everyone to make a deal. Once my buyer and I have made a fair offer and the seller's broker won't budge, I'll get aggressive with the other broker, saying, "This is a fair deal, and you know it. The comps support it. Do you want to lose this sale for your client because you can't be reasonable? Do you want me to call your clients and tell them myself how you're handling this?"

Works all the time.

You also may have noticed that I am never overeager. I hate salespeople who reek of desperation. Even in some universe where it was true, I wouldn't want a potential client to feel like they're the only reason I can keep my lights on. Not chic.

My attitude in listing appointments is that a seller can list their place with me, or not. Regardless of whether they give me their business, I will do them the courtesy of being honest. Their sale isn't going to change my world. Their showing is not going to change my lifestyle. I project the attitude that I don't need their property, even though that seems counterintuitive, *because it builds trust.* If a seller thinks I'm not going to be gaining too much by the sale, they're more likely to take me at my word.

This attitude is kind of like a real estate neg. Hungry salespeople are off-putting. They turn people off. But if I make clients feel like I'm on their level (or richer than them), they're more likely to invest their trust in me. I refer you again to the plastic surgeon example—do you want the doctor who begs for your business, or would you be more confident in the one who doesn't need it?

I always say the best way to sell is not to sell. When I walk into Bloomingdales to buy a pair of underwear, I don't want to be followed by the salesperson (unless it were Betsy Bloomingdale). I don't want to feel like I am being sold something. It's the same thing in real estate. Sell, but don't sell too hard. Not chic.

———— /// ————

FIFTY-FOUR

It's All Negotiable

For me, there are no unwinnable negotiations.

Why?

Because I set myself up for success in every situation. I'm in control of all the aspects of a deal, starting with the most important step of not taking on a client who isn't serious about buying or selling property. In the beginning of my career, I was hesitant about trying to qualify my clients because I was afraid they'd balk if I asked too many questions. My error was conflating asking questions with being pushy.

Spoiler alert: if a client leaves because I try to gauge their commitment to making a deal, I just saved myself a lot of time and heartache.

If I don't start with the solid foundation of a determined buyer/seller, I'm building my house on sand. The structure won't hold; the deal will fall apart once the slightest bit of pressure is applied. I learned this early—and often—as a new broker.

I see red flags when a potential seller tells me, "We just want to put our house out there to see what the market is like." That's not a committed seller. I'd much prefer to hear, "All our kids have left the nest and this house now feels like a museum." Personally, I concentrate on those who express a true need for my services rather than on those with an ephemeral desire to maybe cash in, should the stars align. (Do you see the difference?)

So, how might this translate to your deals?

Let's say you work at a boat dealership. You sell all things marine, from parts for bass trawlers to motor yachts with sleeping cabins. Which client strikes you as more committed to making a purchase: the one who comes in and says, "I'm thinking more horsepower for my bass boat might be nice," or the person who tells you, "I'm on the lake every weekend, and my current motor can't be fixed and I'm itching to replace it so I can get back on the water."

Trick question.

They both could be serious about buying.

(But on the topic of buying a boat . . . don't. The old saying is, the best day in a boat owners life is the day they sell it. I say, if it flies, floats, or fucks, rent it!)

After all, each person took the effort to come into your showroom, and that demonstrates at least a modicum of interest on each of their parts. While it seems like the guy with the specific need for a new motor is the hotter prospect, that's only because you haven't continued to qualify Mr. Horsepower. Why does he want more torque? Do some probing and you'll find out it's because he's looking to upgrade his engine in order to tow a wakeboarder behind his boat.

What you know—and he doesn't—is that his old bass boat, no matter the engine size, can't perform this task. This is where your industry knowledge is crucial. Because you're a student of the boating industry, you can attest that a bass boat can't get up to the speed to lift the wakeboarder out of the water. Mr. Horsepower may come in talking about a new engine, but a skilled salesperson will demonstrate to him that what he wants and needs is a more powerful boat, preferably one with a wakeboard tower.

FLAGG THIS

Knowing your product and industry is a crucial step. If this an area where your deals get hung up, start studying.

Ask for training.

Shadow a more experienced teammate.

Get certified.

Do what it takes to learn more as, ultimately, this factor is within your control.

The next step in closing a deal is where experience comes into play. A good exercise is to reflect on the sales you've made—what did each of them have in common? Are you in an industry that's driven by status and desire, that is, designer handbags, or functionality, like laser printers? Do you sell a commodity, where decisions are almost entirely price driven? Does your customer buy for pleasure? Or security?

The dealmaker's job is to assess and identify what drives clients to make a purchase and tailor the pitch accordingly. We must understand our customers' needs, and we determine them by asking more questions and paying attention to what and how they answer. Only then will we understand the main *why* that will prompt them to write a check or sign a contract. So many amateur salespeople fail to constantly assess needs and make inquiries because they're too busy selling, and then they're puzzled when the deal falls apart for no good reason.

Of course there's a good reason—the dealmaker didn't have all the facts.

For instance, I see too many bad realtors out there, showing homes to young professionals, waxing on about how the guest room can be made into a nursery. But how do they know that children are in the cards for the buyers, now or ever, if they simply assume based on their demographics? That's the lazy way out. It's a shortcut, and shortcuts rarely supersede the results that come from doing the work.

What sets me apart is taking the time to get to know the buying couple. I determine that what they require is enough space to set up two home offices because they're both bosses. That's why they'll buy a home with me, rather than some other broker, even if the other broker charges a lower commission, and even if we show them the same places with the same square footage. I'm selling what accommodates *their* lifestyle. And I know this because I asked all the questions.

What the buyer doesn't realize is, I also ask questions when I already know the answer. There's psychology that comes into play here—they need to hear their own answers, because then I'll use them in my pitch about why this is the perfect house. I don't want my buyers just happy about the decision to buy a house—I need them champing at the bit to write the offer because that will help me power through the negotiation if the seller isn't so flexible.

Once a dealmaker has all the pieces in place, with buyers who are well educated (by me) and excited, the actual negotiations are easy. Closing the deal isn't the time to focus on the home's features and benefits—those should have been determined and cemented far earlier in the sales process.

Making the actual deal is all about hitting the data points in a way that satisfies both the buyers and sellers. If another broker and I have gotten this far in the process, the buyer and seller are both committed, and all parties want it to happen, so it's up to us to find middle ground.

And if somehow we don't, then I get creative and I make the other broker work with me, as now we're a team trying to get a deal done. What can we do to make this happen if we can't land on a satisfactory dollar amount? Can we bypass inspections? Can we do a leaseback? I always have a list of accommodations in my head for when things get dicey. But I often don't need to use them. Ninety-nine times out of one hundred, if I follow all the steps, the deal closes, and all parties are satisfied.

For the one time out of one hundred that it doesn't close?

I use the loss as a learning experience. I retrace every step of the sales process and determine what questions weren't asked and which need wasn't addressed. More often than not, I'm able to determine the cause (*ahem, the other broker*) and accommodate for it in the future. Look at dealmaking like soccer—it's entirely possible that both sides can win.

///

FIFTY-FIVE

Never Say No

There will be times that I know a deal isn't going to close, despite having pulled every trick from my bag. It's disappointing, but it happens. The way I move on *from* this is to move on *to* whatever is next.

I don't let a disappointment slow my trajectory. I don't wallow. I use the failure to stoke my fires. While it never feels like it in the moment, every no is a learning opportunity, even though it may take me a while to appreciate the lesson. (Yes, there are still some lessons I'm waiting to appreciate.)

But here's one piece of advice—when I believe a no is inevitable because the party I represent can't come to terms, let them tell me no. I don't decide for them. I don't give them that out.

For example, let's say I'm representing a buyer who's made their best possible offer on a home and the seller simply can't accept it for whatever reason. The buyer's best offer is $4.5 million and the seller's lowest acceptable price is $5 million, even after the other broker and I have done everything we can to bridge that gap.

In this instance, I will never tell my buyer, "No, it's not happening, and we have to walk away." Instead, I will brief them on the situation, but I won't make their decision for them. They must tell me, "No, it's not happening, and we have to walk away."

Or let's imagine I was in the market for a classic car. Let's say I found what I wanted and the seller and I have negotiated at length. If $100,000 is the point this purchase is no longer a sound investment, I won't budge above that price, even though the seller is looking for more. If I make my best and final offer at $100,000 and he rejects it, I won't tell him I won't go higher. Instead, I'll make him tell me no.

Why would I do this?

First, this puts the onus back onto the other party. I'm not the bad guy here. It's their decision not to move forward, not mine. This shifts the balance of power and can create the feeling of obligation with the other party: "Oh, Josh, we're so sorry, we're going to stay in our current home. But I think our friends might be looking for a bigger place, so let's introduce you."

Second, their disappointment at having to say no can reveal an alternative track. Maybe my buyers decide to tap into a trust to pay the $5 million ask: "You know, we still have that inheritance from Great Aunt Eunice. She would have loved to have seen us in this house." Or maybe the classic car dealer realizes he's being greedy and should accept my generous offer. But if I'm the one to let the buyer or seller off the hook by saying no for them, these alternatives won't be revealed.

By not being the one to say no, I have nothing to lose and something to gain.

PART TEN

///

Realize Your Worth

S elf-doubt can get the best of all of us sometimes, causing us to compare our own worth against that of everyone else. We're all susceptible to feeling down or less than, especially when things go awry.

When this happens, the best way to fight through these feelings is to find a way to remind yourself of all you're capable of achieving.

Or, in the case of some of the cast members of my television show, you're not capable of achieving.

———— /// ————

FIFTY-SIX

The White Whale

I pace anxiously on the bridge overlooking the swans of the Hotel Bel Air. I've waited for this moment for four years. I pinch myself because this feels so surreal.

Am I finally about to meet the woman who's boggled the minds of so many Los Angeles real estate aficionados over the last three decades? The same woman who hasn't been photographed in over thirty years and is worth hundreds of millions of dollars? She who owns some of the most valuable real estate in Los Angeles and yet leaves it abandoned?

I desperately want this dinner to happen, my heart fluttering in uneven beats.

In so many ways, my intended dinner date resembles Huguette Clark, the deceased copper mining heir whose life was the subject of the book *Empty Mansions*. All her properties, full of art and treasure, laid fallow until her death, as she chose to live in Doctors Hospital for twenty years instead of in her 5th Avenue thirty-room Manhattan mansion in the sky or her palace on the Pacific. Or her estate in Santa Barbara worth hundreds of millions of dollars.

Fifteen minutes passes but no one shows. Have I missed her? Did she come early and go to the restaurant without me?

I decide to check, proceeding on unsteady legs.

I chose the restaurant because of the privacy it affords. Surely some-one as reclusive as her would value my discretion.

There's a light breeze attempting to muss my hair (unsuccessful), the scent of rain in the air. I walk up the three steps, hand on the brass railing. I step inside the Hotel Bel Air and head to the bar, drawn in by delectable scents of food and the din of whispered conversations.

The hostess stands at her station, her expression open and pleasant. She smiles as I approach. "Can I help you, Mr. Flagg?"

"Yes, I was wondering—I'm sorry this is going to sound so strange, but I was supposed to meet someone out front," I say, vaguely waving to the bridge across the street. "I was wondering if maybe they'd already come in and were waiting for me here."

"What does she look like?"

I flash her a nervous grin. "That's the strange part. I don't know. I've never met her before."

"Oh, how interesting."

But I can tell she finds this less "interesting" and more "crazy." Am I crazy? I'm starting to second-guess myself.

I glance into the restaurant, patrons eating and talking. I notice two tables with single women and wonder if one of them might be her. I offer a nod; you know the one—it's the awkward looking nod, the one you hope they answer with a nod of their own but . . . no. Neither one of them offer a nod in return.

Shit.

I thank the hostess and wander back to the bridge, checking my watch. I'll give it a bit more time. It's been four years—surely I can spare a few more minutes.

The night has turned cool, the breeze picking up, the sun dipping lower in the horizon. I shiver and notice the colors spreading across the sky, like spilled paint.

I wait. Then I wait some more. I'm considering going back to my place, sitting by the fire and sipping a cordial, but that would feel like defeat.

Shit, she's not coming, is she?

Now, it's almost 7:00 p.m. and I still haven't gotten a response to my texts. I'm about to call it quits. I'm not going to spend all night out here, even though that's what my heart wants me to do. She stood me up.

I'm not going to lie: I'm devastated.

Occasionally after a professional disappointment, I'll start to question my own choices. Maybe a listing appointment doesn't go my way. Maybe a buyer chooses a different broker. Maybe a deal falls apart, despite my best efforts. Maybe a client cheats me out of a commission. Maybe I don't get to have dinner with the West Coast Huguette Clark.

I am gutted. I want to direct my fury somewhere, but with no one to blame, I turn it back on myself.

In these quiet moments when I'm alone, I'll wonder why even I do what I do. Is this it? Real estate? I mean, is this the best I can do? Why did I pick a job that isn't considered impressive by most people? Couldn't I have been an art dealer, working for Christie's instead? Sure, I'm at the far end of the bell curve in terms of success, but there are plenty of my peers who willingly pay to slap their faces on shopping carts. (I mean, I can't. I just can't.) I don't love that we're members of the same weird, not chic fraternity.

When the negative thoughts appear, I admit it—I will begin to rabbit-hole, spiraling into doubt and discontent.

Then I'll begin to wonder why there are so many television shows about real estate. Real estate is not inherently as glamourous or prestigious as some professions, like hedge fund managers or lawyers. And what I do isn't nearly as impressive as being a physician. They save lives; I find properties with an extra powder room. I realize this is more of an existential question. I contemplated asking Bravo why all these programs exist, but I don't want them to be all, "Yeah, why *do* we have this show?"

According to a Gallup poll, realtors rank among America's least-trusted professions. Only 20 percent of respondents found us trustworthy. Ouch.

Christ, I'm a bummer.

This isn't who I am; I need to snap out of it.

Here's the thing—I know it's okay to have an occasional concern about my career, about myself, about my direction. Even the best of us suffers from occasional self-doubt.

Maybe I seem like I'm full of bravado, but there are days when everything goes wrong and I'm left wanting, dragged down by negative thoughts. But everything else about today was great—this is one bad moment in a day full of good moments, productive moments, lucrative moments. Moments when I was proud of myself, of my team, of what we've built.

When I start to feel this way, I remind myself to push past these feelings and understand that they are temporary. Again, it's normal to wallow when disappointed. Depression is a human emotion and can strike regardless of how rosy the circumstances. (I know this for a fact . . . I'm on a ton of antidepressants and employ three different shrinks. I am quite confident I put two of their kids through college and may have bought another one a lake house.)

I realize I'm preemptively mourning the loss, assuming Anastasia wants nothing to do with me, when I have no conclusive evidence that this is the case. Folks, this is also called rumination . . . when you repeat over and over and over in your mind the same thing and ask yourself the same questions again and again.

What's most helpful when I start feeling like this is to take a step away from myself and remind myself how my efforts have helped others. When I really get into a rare funk, I double down on my charitable giving. I volunteer my services. I must remember that I'm working for causes greater than that of my own enjoyment, amusement, and enrichment.

Because of what I do, I can do good work. I make a difference.

In melancholic moments, this knowledge anchors me. This is when I tell myself that it doesn't matter if selling real estate is chic; it's what I do. It's who I am. I've created a position for myself that's been my fate since I was a child, and every day I enjoy the hell out of it. My job not only gives me a lifestyle I love but is the conduit for my providing for others. And damn it, I can be chic while doing it, exactly the way I believe it should be done.

Darker thoughts will always appear; I recognize that. No matter who you are, no matter what you do, they are inevitable. The key is to make ourselves remember that these thoughts are fleeting and should be treated as such. When I try to envision myself in another career, I get twitchy. I hate the idea of waking up in the morning and doing anything differently. (Also, the money is too good . . . I would not enjoy earning less; I'm confident of this.)

That's when I realize that I'm exactly where I need to be, working the career I've been training for my whole life.

This right job/right place realization has been tantamount in maintaining the million-dollar mindset, because the mindset is entirely mental. The mindset can't be achieved if I don't love what I do at least 85 percent of the time. When I falter or flag during that 15 percent of my downtime, I must remind myself of all the good my passion has fueled. I must recall and embrace why I got into the business, why I leapfrogged right over college so I could immediately begin to live my dreams, to meet my destiny, because that knowledge will keep me on the path to success.

As a dealmaker, I'm here by choice.

We dealmakers are all here by choice.

We're here because we've made a commitment to earn the life we want.

We're here because we're worthy.

Our only trajectory is onward, pulling ourselves—and others—upward, on to whatever is next.

So, I'm going to shake off this loss and move on with my day.

On the bright side, my hair still looks perfect, so I decide to turn my lemons into lemonade and put them into vodka. I shall have a drink. I'm here, I may as well enjoy myself.

I'm about to make my way in and order a martini as a car pulls up. The driver's side of a ten-year-old Ford pickup truck opens. A woman exits and crosses the 400 block of Stone Canyon and enters the hotel.

The woman approaches me. She appears to be in her midsixties. Standing about five feet four inches tall, she's wearing a face mask adorned with the flag of Mexico on it, with glasses neatly framing her face, her hair gathered up around her head.

It's her.

Holy shit, *it's her.*

The only known photograph of this woman is from the mid-1980s when she was wearing the same glasses while doting on the three children she and Mr. Beaverhausen had together.

She approaches me, removing her mask. "Josh? I'm Ana."

I don't know what to say for a few seconds, such is my shock. She is actually standing right in front of me. How can this be? Forgetting all about personal boundaries in a post-COVID world, I automatically reach my hand out to her, which she shakes.

I say, "Ana, it's so wonderful to meet you. Would you like to go inside to the restaurant and have a cocktail?"

She grins at me; her smile is beautiful, lighting up the whole night. I offer my own in response.

"Sure, I'd like that."

We make our way to the bar, and I'm in a daze the whole time, just completely starstruck.

After we're seated with drinks ordered, she turns to me and gives me a light tap on the wrist, saying the most magical words I've ever heard.

"So, Josh, what's next?"

ACKNOWLEDGMENTS

———— /// ————

I've been practicing my Academy Award acceptance speech since I was a child. As I've not acted since grade school theater camp at Greystone, my Oscar seems somewhat less inevitable now (but not impossible, never impossible). Regardless, please imagine me acknowledging all of the involved while standing at a podium, clad in a bespoke tux as Meryl beams from the front row. Here's what the notecard I'd hold in my excited, shaking hands would read: First, for Edith Flagg, the best person I ever met, as well as the most influential. I live my life to make you proud.

Much love and admiration to my parents, Michael and Cindy Flagg; you created all this, and I am forever in your debt. I will absolutely make sure you end up in a nursing home.

For Claire Jenkins and Hilary Markus Kelly, you are the Mussolinis that keep the trains of my life running on time. Shouting "Next!" to you is an honor and a privilege—unless and until you shank me for it. I'd still love you after, though.

Olimpia, I would be lost without you and I adore you like family because you are family. (Maybe even more so, as you're here by choice.) Do I like that George loves you more than me? No. But I get it and I don't blame him.

For my partner in crime, Jen Lancaster, thank you for keeping me in line and editing me appropriately. Ten points for removing every Fatty Arbuckle reference. In a perfect world, I'd take you to France and buy you a pre-owned Birkin bag (but I probably won't).

For Robert Evans, amazing how someone I never met could have such an influence on my life. Rest in power, Kid Notorious.

Big love to my Bravo family, especially my BFFs, Josh Altman and Tracy Tutor. You are the rising tides that raise all boats. And for the World of Wonder team, you're simply the best.

Much respect and admiration to Steve Troha and Katherine Odom-Tomchin of Folio Literary. Thanks so much for recognizing my potential and guiding this ship.

Major thanks to my editor Sara Kendrick at HarperCollins Leadership, as well as David McNeill, and David Wienir—I hope you had as much fun with this process as I did. (Sorry if I made you pull out your own hair at any point.) (I refer you to the deleted Fatty Arbuckle sections.) And much appreciation to everyone on board who makes books happen, from editorial to marketing to publicity to sales; I'm in awe of what you do.

To my clients, thank you for letting me work a career I'd happily do for free. (Okay, not for free.) I live my dream because you believe in me, so thank you.

I have been blessed with the most amazing group of friends, so all my love to Candy Spelling, Melissa Rivers, Nikki Haskell, Roxy Bijan, Heather McDonald, Heather Altman, Carly Steel, Jeff Lewis, Tori Spelling, Paula Abdul, Bruce Vilanch, Rick Caruso, Warren Beatty, Sonja Morgan, Kathy Yedor, Adam Rubin, Carrie Brillstein, Amy Weiss, Zach Zalben, and Matt Kornberg. There's a dinner party in our near future.

Well, I hear the orchestra cueing up, so I have to wrap this up with one last thank you—to my fans and social media followers, I love you for "getting" me and hope I've done my best to keep you entertained.

INDEX

Maui, 95, 96
mavens, 67
Mayfair Carriage Co., 116
McDonald, Heather, 122
Mentor, 67
Mercedes-Benz Roadster (author's car),
     116–17
MGM, 71
Microsoft, 118
"Millionaire Mile" (Los Angeles), 25
Million Dollar Listing Los Angeles (TV
     show), 35, 36, 54, 102, 125, 167,
     194–96
million-dollar mindset, 3–7
mindset, 3–7, 87–88, 108–11, 208–9
Minkoff, Crystal Kung, 185
mistakes, learning from your, 102–7, 133,
     137
mitzvah, 206, 208
mold, 190
money
     and happiness, 7
     spending, 125–30
Montcalm Avenue (Los Angeles), 154–56
Monte Carlo, 116
Montecito (Santa Barbara neighborhood),
     79, 122
Morgan, Sonja, 13
motivation, and action, 87, 203
"Mr. Mentor" (broker), 20–23, 39,
     41–44
"Mrs. Indecisive" (client), 189–92
Mulholland Drive (Los Angeles), 154
multitasking, 26
Murray, Bill, 105–6

Nazis, 117, 198–200
negative traits, utilizing your, 29
negotiating
     being tough in, 4, 6
     flexibility in, 233–36
     high-end deals, 113–14
     from a position of strength, 135, 136,
        229–32

neighbors, visiting the, 161
Neiman Marcus, 36, 200
nemesis, finding a, 194–97
nepotism, 90
Netflix, 8
networking
     and confidence, 86
     and face time, 183–85
     with friends, 122–24
     by knocking on people's doors, 108–11
     and making an entrance, 94–96
     and opening lines, 92–93
New York, 176
New York Post, 17
New York Times, 115
"no"
     letting the buyer say, 237–38
     when to say, 131, 133–39
nonverbal cues, 26
North Alpine Drive (Los Angeles), 52

offer(s)
     and overcoming small gaps, 230–31
     refusing the first, 219–20
     strategies for, 224–28
older clients, 101
Old Hollywood, 155
Olimpia (author's housekeeper), 13
Onassis, Jacqueline Kennedy, 11
O'Neal, Shaquille, 6
open houses, brokers', 105
opening lines, 92–93
Outliers (Gladwell), 9
overeager, avoiding appearing, 231

Pacific Design Center, 200
Pacific Palisades (Los Angeles), 122, 123
Palm Springs, Calif., 17, 133–35, 137
passions, identifying your, 12
patterns, recognizing, 95, 215
People magazine, 17
Perry, Matthew, 178
personal touch, adding the, 66–68
philanthropy, 7, 205–9

ABOUT THE AUTHOR

———— /// ————

JOSH FLAGG is best known as the original cast member on the Bravo show *Million Dollar Listing: Los Angeles* (although the youngest on the show, he has appeared from the beginning) and for his decade's worth of high-end deals in the Beverly Hills real estate industry. He's sold more than $2.5 billion worth of property and is among the top five real estate agents in all of Los Angeles. His record-selling achievements include the sale of style icon and Los Angeles socialite Betsy Bloomingdale's Holmby Hills estate for $40 million and the most expensive house ever sold in The Flats of Beverly Hills.

Josh has sold homes to many exclusive clients, including A-List celebrities and high-net-worth individuals such as Adam Levine, Shonda Rhimes, and Steve Aoki, and illustrious Los Angeles families like the Gettys and Debartolos. He also represents some of the city's most notable builders, developers, business managers, and attorneys. He's constantly setting new records—recognized by the *Wall Street Journal* as one of the top-ranked agents in California as well as nationally, and listed on the *Forbes* "30 under 30" most influential people in their industries. Flagg has been covered many times by *Variety* and the *Hollywood Reporter* and resides in Beverly Hills.